Let Go

Let Go

Rewire your subconscious mind with hypnosis & cure material addiction – Real Life Stories

BY

KURT GASSNER

My-mindguide.com

Let Go
Kurt Gassner

Impressum
My-mindguide – The publishing trademarke of trendguide Capital GmbH, Klenzestr. 42a, 80469 Munich, Germany.

Reg. Nr. HRB Munich 206639, VAT 152 123 159, CEO: Kurt Friedrich Gassner
Web: www.my-mindguide.com, mail: gassner@my-mindguide.com

Paperback ISBN: 978-3-98793-999-0
Ebook ISBN: 978-3-949978-47-0
Hardback ISBN: 978-3-949978-46-3

Table of Contents

Materialism

My-mindguide.com

Materialisim
My-mindguide.com

INTRODUCTION

Would you like a long-term solution to your addictions? Do you ever feel imprisoned, working so hard to get your life back on track only to fall off the wagon again and again? Do you require immediate assistance? If you responded "Yes!" to any of these questions, hypnosis may be the solution you've been looking for.

There is currently no clear agreement among health experts on how to define addiction. It has historically been characterized only in terms of psychoactive substances such as alcohol, cigarettes and so on, but numerous professionals have recently made note of other abnormal behavioral patterns that are not specifically substance-based. These addictions include gambling, eating, sex, pornography, computers, video games, TV, dieting, social media, job, exercise, shopping, self-mutilation, and indeed *materialism*.

The victims of all of these diseases have one thing in common: they are internally compelled to engage in the particular behavior that characterizes their addiction in an intense and repetitive manner.

Furthermore, modern neuroscience research suggests that the neurophysiology of all addictive illnesses, whether substance- or behavioral-based, is strikingly similar in many ways. Endorphins (or endogenous morphine) are a common mediator in all of these illnesses, as are essential transmitter substances including dopamine, adrenaline, and serotonin.

In today's environment, the incidence of these addictions is alarmingly high. In the United States alone, 15.1 million people are addicted to alcohol; four million are addicted to drugs, and more than 20% of the population is addicted to tobacco.

Although there is no reliable way to estimate the total prevalence of all the behavioral addictions, there is abundant evidence that they are extremely common. As a matter of fact, there are probably very few people alive today who are not subject to some form of addictive behavior.

The excellent news is, there is hope for everyone, even those who have endured an addiction to materialism for years. Nowadays, there are manifold treatment possibilities such as therapy, support groups, and intensive programs. Most people turn to professionals for help—doctors, counselors, and hypnotherapists.

Hypnotherapists have now been granted access to modern medicine. More and more individuals are turning to hypnosis to help them quit smoking, fight drug or alcohol addiction, conquer fears and phobias, and discover a permanent treatment for depression and anxiety problems. Hypnotherapy has been shown to be particularly effective for weight loss in trials. Patients all around the world have benefited from the introduction of hypnosis as an alternative treatment.

High-tech hypnotherapy works by reprogramming your subconscious mind as a means to solve your health problems. The amazing part about this form of treatment is that it goes beyond the surface to address the underlying problem. Regaining control of your life begins with resolving your problem at its root. Once you do so, it will be much simpler for you to break away from your bad habits and live the life you have always desired.

In this case, answering the following question truthfully will help you figure out whether you suffer an addiction: Do I ever feel compelled to engage in any type of behavior that I consider to be self-defeating or destructive, and for which I later experience guilt, humiliation, embarrassment, and/or remorse?

REFERENCES

**REAL-LIFE STORY ABOUT MATERIAL ADDICTION
(my friend Fred)**

For some years now, I have been the biggest cheerleader of the "shop now, pay later" scheme—Afterpay.

If you know me personally, you know that I have used and loved this notion of "responsible spending" since the launch of the business in 2015.

Quite frankly, I don't even remember a time without it . . . and that's the problem.

I'll never forget when I discovered its existence and thinking about what an amazing idea it was (but also annoyed that I didn't dream it up first).

It was exactly what I needed—a guilt-free way of spreading out my purchases over a period of time to make it more financially manageable. The world was my spending oyster as far as I was concerned.

I could never understand why people were so against the business because it just made SO much sense to me, and to an extent, it still does!

My advocacy for the fortnightly-scheduled payments never wavered. It became annoying to me when people would question my spending habits, tell me I didn't need to purchase what I had, or laugh at my constant use of the app.

"They just don't understand," I used to say to myself. "If I were earning as much as them, I wouldn't need to use this!"

There wasn't a single doubt in my mind about my use or dependency on this app. None whatsoever.

That was, until I'd be left with nothing. Nothing. Not a single cent. Not even enough to buy myself a coffee in the morning with a staff discount (that's $3).

At that point, I physically couldn't spend money normally anymore; everything I was purchasing was being divided into four payments in my mind. I was totally incapable of spending my money responsibly.

I was an addict. I was completely addicted to spending money and engulfed in the feeling of having everything I wanted. If you search the definition of being an addict, it's characterised as an "enthusiastic devotee," but I knew that it was more than that.

Growing up, I never wanted to miss out on anything, no matter what it was. I always wanted to be included in plans, invited to birthdays, and immersed in the latest trends.

It was always so exciting to me when I had more to offer than the next person because it made me feel cool. To this day, the need for acceptance has never left me, and I can admit that about myself.

I suffered a lot from the fear of missing out, and this notion has now spiralled into my adulthood.

And then came the credit card.

I'm sure you can imagine how damaging this was to my spending habits. "It's just for emergency purposes and bills," I said, over and over again.

I'll never forget the day when my pay came in, and quite literally every single dollar had to go toward paying off my credit card and Afterpay installments.

It was more than humiliating.

There wouldn't go a day where I wouldn't see people I know on social media buying houses, and yet here I was with not a cent to my name because I couldn't control myself. The only "credit" that I would give *myself* is that I was always really strict with paying back what I owed.

You know those people that say they woke up one day and decided to make a change? At last, my day came.

Over the course of this isolation period, I started to recognize my bad behaviours and understand why I had dug a hole so deep. Whether it was a matter of self-justification or to feel a certain high, I knew it all had to stop, as the stress was quite literally eating me alive.

So, I decided I'd had enough.

My Afterpay and Zippay accounts are fully paid off and closed. My credit card is paid off, cut up, and never to be opened again. It's been an expensive lesson, and one that I don't wish to learn again. The feeling of freedom is second to none.

I've always been one of those people that have lived in the now and enjoyed the moment, but I never thought about the repercussions. The shift in learned behaviour is going to be hard, but oh my God is it going to be worth it.

One of the big motivators throughout all of this has been my ability to consult a therapist after I made up my mind to fight and get over every form of addiction in my life—a therapist who could share similar experiences and discuss money goals that I aspire to.

Hypnotherapy has been a massive driving force to this change, and I would highly recommend it to others who find themselves combatting any form of addiction.

I'm so excited to build a financial future for myself.

MATERIALISM ADDICTIONS

To be materialistic means to have values that put a relatively high priority on money, having possessions, and popularity.

I think materialism is viewed in a negative light because people may have had unpleasant experiences with materialistic people. We know from research that materialism tends to be associated with treating others in more competitive, manipulative and selfish ways, as well as with being less empathetic. Such behavior usually isn't appreciated by the average person, although it is encouraged by some aspects of our capitalist economic system.

Research shows two sets of factors that lead people to have materialistic values. First, people are more materialistic when they are exposed to messages that suggest such pursuits are important, whether through their parents and friends, society, or the media. Second—and somewhat less obviously—people are more materialistic when they feel insecure or threatened, whether because of rejection, economic fears, or thoughts of their own death.

Simply put, materialism is the importance one places on material possessions. These possessions could be anything, such as clothes, shoes, handbags, cars, electronic equipment, and gadgets. One's home also counts as a material control, even though everyone needs a place to live. Materialistic people don't view their home as a mere place of comfort and shelter; it also reflects their social status in some way.

Someone with a high level of materialism, described as "materialistic," considers material possessions to be central to their life and their identity. They focus a good deal of their energy on acquiring possessions. Someone with a low level of materialism, described as "non-materialistic," doesn't consider acquiring possessions to be particularly important, although they vary in the extent to which they acquire material possessions in order to meet other objectives, such as social acceptance.

A NEW WAY TO UNDERSTAND ADDICTIONS

The following formulation, although grossly oversimplified in many ways, is intended to provide an initial framework for understanding how basic mindfulness offers a highly effective way to deconstruct the brain/mind formations that underlie all addictive behaviors.

Like all other creatures on this planet, humans universally tend to seek pleasure and to avoid or escape from pain. Although these two extremely strong genetic instincts have been and continue to be essential to survival, they are also the extremely fertile common ground in which all addictive behaviors become strongly rooted and sustained.

The basic habit patterns that comprise the core of these addictions start developing out of our intrinsic propensities in a very natural and lawful way before we're born and continue to proliferate from that point onward.

The twin principles that govern their natural initial development can be stated quite simply, although they progressively evolve into highly complex and subtle brain/mind processes that are much more challenging to understand.

Principle #1:
Whenever we do anything that is followed by an increase in subjective pleasure or satisfaction, the probability that we will do it again increases to some degree. In general, the probability of recurrence of such a behavior is proportional to the degree of pleasure/satisfaction experienced.

Each subsequent repetition of this particular sequence further increases the probability of its future recurrence or its "habit strength." As it continues to develop, it will tend to become increasingly streamlined or "automatic," requiring progressively less conscious awareness and/or intentionality for its occurrence. An automatic habit pattern that has developed primarily in this way will be referred to here as a pleasure-seeking reaction.

Principle #2:
Whenever we do anything that is followed by a decrease in subjective physical/emotional pain, discomfort, or dissatisfaction, the probability that we will do it again also increases slightly. Again, this increment in the probability of

recurrence is generally proportional to the degree of reduction in subjective pain/dissatisfaction that is experienced.

Each subsequent repetition of this sequence similarly increases the probability of its future recurrence or its "habit strength." As this happens, it will also become progressively more automatic as described above. This type of automatic habit pattern will be referred to here as a terminating reaction.

As used above, the words, "do anything," refer to external behaviors as well as their internal representations (i.e., the emotional feelings, mental imagery and/or self-talk to which they give rise). Typically, these internal representations are strongly linked to the external behavioral reactions from which they are derived and thus become a key part of the overall reactive pattern. Very commonly, they also play an important part in activating the external behavioral aspect of the reaction.

For example, thinking about/imaging a piece of chocolate cake in the refrigerator will tend to activate the corresponding pleasure-seeking reaction of actually eating it. Similarly, if you, have a headache, your terminating reaction of taking an aspirin is highly likely to be preceded by thinking, for example, "I need an aspirin" and/or an image of taking one and getting relief.

As nearly everyone knows from much personal experience, reliving a pleasure-seeking reaction in imagery tends to activate—at least to some degree—subtle feelings of pleasure; conversely, reliving a terminating reaction in imagery tends to activate subtle feelings of getting relief from pain/discomfort.

The same is truc of anticipatory imagery and/or engaging in internal self-talk about future occurrences of pleasure or pain.

For example, someone experiencing a lot of stress at work may repeatedly imagine what they going to do when the weekend comes and/or think repetitiously, "I can hardly wait to . . ." Both of these internal processes can be understood as subtle, garden-variety internal terminating reactions. It's very important to understand that they also commonly occur automatically and beyond the bounds of our conscious awareness.

Within this framework, then, an addictive behavior can be defined as any pleasure-seeking reaction, terminating reaction, or a combination of both that is significantly harmful to oneself and/or others and that has become sufficiently strong and automatic enough to effectively override—at least on some occasions—one's intentionally conscious efforts to suppress or control it.

By this definition, all addictions cause physical and/or emotional pain; and since pain tends to activate automatic terminating reactions, this sets up a self-perpetuating process or "vicious cycle."

Consider, for example, an alcoholic who chronically worries about how to pay his bills and who has had a highly stressful week at work. Predictably, this triggers a strong terminating reaction of stopping for "happy hour" at his favorite bar, where he ends up getting drunk, spending a large part of his paycheck, and staying until the bar closes.

His wife, expecting him to come home to participate in a special birthday celebration for one of their children, becomes very emotionally upset, as do all of the children. They are traumatized further by the loud argument that ensues between their parents after he finally gets home.

When he wakes up the next morning, he has a terrible hangover and is filled with intense guilt, shame, and self-loathing about what he has done. His baseline level of emotional pain, which he temporarily terminated through ingesting a large amount of alcohol, has now increased tremendously—far above its original high base level.

Given this level of pain, it is highly likely that the same terminating reaction will be quickly reactivated, setting off another addictive round in this tragic circle.

INTERNET ADDICTION AND MATERIALISM

Materialism is defined as "the importance a consumer attaches to worldly possessions." In other words, in common usage, materialism is associated with the tendency to consider material possessions and physical comfort more important than spiritual values—and due to globalization, individual levels of materialism are on the rise. A study conducted by the UCLA/American Council of Education that surveyed a quarter-million collegians, and the proportion of individuals who expressed financial success as very important to them grew from 39 percent in 1970 to 78 percent in 2009. Like loneliness, several negative consequences of materialism have been noted. For instance, risk-taking behavior and ethical lapses are common among materialistic CEOs. In general, it has been found that materialism is negatively associated with one's wellbeing, which is based on a recent meta-analytic study that consisted of 259 independent samples. Likewise, materialism has been commonly associated with psychological disorders such as anxiety and depression, compulsive buying, and risky health behaviors such as smoking cigarettes, drinking alcohol, and using drugs. Furthermore, materialism and loneliness have been considered to be associated with each other. For instance, Pieters noted that materialism and loneliness tend to influence each other in a downward spiral mode.

Some research has addressed the relationship between behavioral addiction and materialism. For example, it has been noted that materialism positively predicts smartphone addiction, which is similar to Internet addiction. Also, other studies have noted the role of materialism in the context of Internet addiction. It has been posited that further exploration between materialism and Internet addiction is warranted. Therefore, based on limited literature, the following hypothesis is proposed:

Materialism is positively associated with Internet addiction as well.

WHY MATERIALISM IS MAKING YOU UNHAPPY

Materialists lead unhappier lives and are worse to the people around them. And it seems that social media might be fueling materialistic attitudes, too.

Materialists tend to be sad people, indeed.

We know from substantial research that materialism tends to be associated with treating others in more competitive, manipulative, and selfish ways, as well as with being less empathy.

Materialism is associated with lower levels of well-being, less pro-social interpersonal behavior, more ecologically destructive behavior, and worse academic outcomes. It is also is associated with more spending problems and debt.

We found that the more highly people endorsed materialistic values, the more they experienced unpleasant emotions, depression and anxiety. Additionally, they reported more physical health problems, such as stomachaches and headaches, and they less frequently experienced pleasant emotions and satisfaction in their lives.

People become more materialistic when they feel insecure.

Research shows two sets of factors that lead people to have materialistic values. First, people are more materialistic when they are exposed to messages that suggest such pursuits are important. Second, people are more materialistic when they feel insecure or threatened, whether because of rejection, economic fears, or thoughts of their own death.

Materialism is linked to media exposure and national-advertising expenditures as well:

Research shows that the more that people watch television, the more materialistic their values tend to be. A study recently published with psychologist Jean Twenge found that the extent to which a given year's class of high school seniors cared about materialistic pursuits was predictable on the basis of how much of the US economy came from advertising and marketing expenditures. The more that advertising dominated the economy, the more materialistic youth were.

Materialism is linked to social media use, too.

One study of American and Arab youth found that materialism is higher as social media use increases. That makes sense, since most social media messages also contain advertising, which is how the social media companies make a profit.

Many psychologists believe that materialists are unhappy because these people neglect their real psychological needs.

Materialistic values are associated with living one's life in ways that do a relatively poor job of satisfying psychological needs to feel free, competent, and connected to other people. When people do not have their needs well-satisfied, they report lower levels of well-being and happiness, as well as more distress.

REASONS WHY PEOPLE BECOME OBSESSED WITH MATERIAL POSSESSIONS

Improving Our Self-Image
Nearly all of us care about how other people see us to a certain extent.

Many of these concerns are perfectly healthy and normal, such as wanting others to see us as trustworthy, caring, and generally "good." Of course, what truly matters is that we actually *are* these things.

Many people care about less healthy aspects of their self-image, though. We want to be seen as cool, trendy, wealthy, successful and all of the other nuances that come with them.

In the pursuit of this self-image, it's expected that some people will become obsessed with material possessions. For example:

- Buying a luxury-brand car when a more normal brand is sufficient or what's truly affordable.

- Buying brand-name clothes for the sole purpose of brand reputation (e.g., buying a $300 belt when a $40 model works just as well).

- Shopping at "trendy" (but pricier) stores for supplies like groceries for the self-image it supposedly brings, when regular stores have plenty to offer for less. Not naming names but you probably have ideas of your own!

- Socializing at expensive clubs, bars, restaurants, and other exotic locales that are extremely expensive. The real issue arises when a person spends far more money than they responsibly should to go to these places.

- Scraping money together to live in a more upscale neighborhood is a common way people get trapped by wanting to be seen as a "success," particularly in high-rent areas like NYC, Boston, San Francisco and other major cities. Not picking on them—they're beautiful and awesome in their own ways—but many make the mistake of trying to live beyond their means,

Expecting That Material Possessions Will Boost Our Social Status

Humans are social creatures by nature (via NCBI). We can't help it. It's how we're wired, and it's been the way we've lived since tribal eras of the past. When socializing in groups, a social hierarchy typically emerges, regardless of geographic location, demographic, or time period.

In many cases, a social hierarchy serves a purpose. According to *Science Direct*, a social hierarchy emerges naturally in people and animals alike to provide some kind of order, ranking, system of conflict resolution, and organization. In short, social hierarchies, psychologically speaking, are meant to avoid chaos at their core.

Of course, there are many nuances and factors that come into play due to our consciences and higher cognitive abilities. Humans in modern times understand that teamwork, social balancing, good intentions, merit, helping others and intelligence are also key factors regarding where one falls in a hierarchy.

Here's a powerful excerpt from an article titled "Neuroimaging Investigations of Social Status and Social Hierarchies":

…in some instances, status-based hierarchies can incentivize those lower in relative rank to progress and achieve higher standing among their peers, thus providing motivation to perform a variety of behaviors.

We believe that this is a major explanation behind why some people become obsessed with material possessions – they're actually obsessed with where they fall on a perceived social hierarchy.

Recapping from earlier, material possessions can cover lifestyle choices, neighborhoods we live in, where we go, what we do and becoming part of a club or group in addition to typical possessions. Perhaps you think of people you know who embody this mindset in terms of these items . . .

Competition Amongst Family, Friends, and Peers
You've probably heard the expression "keeping up with the Joneses" before. Courtesy of Wikipedia, we've learned that the expression comes from a comic strip of the same name, which was published in 1913 by Arthur R. Momand.

In short, the premise of the comic is centered on a family who struggles to keep up with their neighbors ("the Joneses") in a variety of social and economic ways.

The vast majority of us have fallen victim to the "keeping up with the Joneses" mentality at some point. This effect can happen in relation to our neighbors but also friends, coworkers, in-laws and many others in our community. The effect even takes place on social media apps like Instagram, where we try to be more like influencers and celebrities.

This competition between us and people we know can drive many of the decisions we make.

Our brother or sister went on three exotic vacations with their family last year? We want to have the same experiences for ourselves.

The nextdoor neighbors renovate the outside of their house. Guess who's now thinking about how much it'll cost to upgrade theirs?

Our close friend buys a German sports car. Our reliable ten-year old sedan that we normally love feels like driving a Playskool car in comparison.

We could go on and on, but you get the idea. The competition among our peers can make us become even more obsessed with material possessions in order to feel good enough, worthy of or even better than our peers.

Shopping and Buying Things Is a Thrill
To some of us, shopping is a thrill. For others, buying new things is an addiction.

There's something fun about buying new stuff for many people. A desire arises for something new. Perhaps a sibling gets a new "toy," or we see a social media influencer repping a new brand. We decide that we must have one, too.

The excitement overcomes us as we browse the Internet or head to the store. We finally buy 'the thing' and it's great.

There's a rush over the newness of our newest purchase. We ride the high of taking that car out for a spin or wearing our new jewelry to a party.

Then, the inevitable happens. That car loses its luster. Our new shirt stays in the closet for weeks. No one ever uses that hot tub anymore!

As quickly as it came, the rush we got from buying something new is gone. We return to our original state . . . that is, until we get the urge to buy another new thing.

This process is called "hedonic adaptation"—also knew as the "Hedonic Treadmill"—and no one is exempt. There are two reasons why hedonic adaptation is so tricky to deal with:

It's random. We can't control when the urge to shop will hit us, nor where the influence comes from.

Feelings are tough to ignore. It takes serious discipline—both in terms of fighting our feelings and in terms of budgeting—to not give in when the urge to shop hits us.

The good news? The first steps are to simply be aware of our urges and to observe our feelings. When we're aware of it, we begin to separate ourselves from it. We must control ourselves.

Next, we recommend setting up a budget and sticking to it firmly!

Expecting Material Possessions to Bring Us Happiness
Ah, chasing happiness. We all want to be happy . . . but how? Here are some thoughts that most of us has have had at some point . . .

- "Once I get the big promotion, I'll be happy." Until then, we believe we can't be as happy.
- "Once I buy a house, I can really enjoy life." As of now, any happiness we feel is simply not as good as it could be.
- "Once I find a partner, I'll feel complete." For now, we're just going to anxiously wait for them to come along.

See a pattern emerging here? We oftentimes base our happiness on external circumstances.

Being obsessed with material things is no different. Suppose we aren't feeling satisfied in life. In that case, it can be easy to pin it on something we think is missing: a better car, making more money, new clothes, a bigger house, taking expensive trips, having a certain type of social group, you name it.

If you're holding off on feeling happy until the "big ticket" comes, we've got some bad news: it's not all it's cracked up to be.

There's even an expression that comes with it: "The curse of the lottery."

Of course, a healthy, balanced person can do great things and enjoy life with their winnings. The irony is this: these people don't need to win the lottery to be happy in the first place!

Influence of Elders and Mentors at an Early Age
Many of us become obsessed with material possessions, as we've defined them, in our formative years. It doesn't always look like how one might expect, either.

Typical examples can come in the form of our parents expecting us to attend a certain school, have a specific type of friends, and get a particular job. Elders around us may expect us to maintain a certain socio-economic standing and to impress others through material means.

The opposite can also happen.

For those of us who grow up poor, we might rather die than live the way we did when we were kids. Some people experience shame, guilt and embarrassment by their lack of means as children and want nothing more than to overcome the plight of their parents, which can come in many forms. We tell ourselves that, no matter what, we'll never live like that.

Many famous musicians and athletes can be placed in this category. Their drive to overcome their circumstances or family image in early years is what pushes them to reach success—and show that success through material means, too.

Whether our parents intentionally lead us down the path of materialism or indirectly through their own actions, our early years absolutely play a role in our materialism and consumerism.

Coping With Fear of Our Mortality

Time to get a little dark. All of our time in this world is limited. It's the great equalizer. No one is exempt, and there's no way to avoid it.

That said, some of us try our hardest to fight this fact. One of the ways we do this is by becoming extremely attached to what we have in this lifetime. This includes an attachment to material things.

If we make enough money, reach a certain status, or possess all sorts of material things, perhaps we can forget about the finite nature of life. Perhaps we can bring these things with us to the afterlife!

Humans have been thinking like this for millennia. Pharaohs were frequently buried with their riches in ancient Egypt. A similar practice was common at Norse funerals.

In either case, many people sacrifice quite a bit to obtain these material possessions, thinking that it's necessary for life to have meaning or worth. Given that life is temporary, though, one begins to wonder what's being sacrificed when we make material things our top priority in life.

ESCAPING MATERIALISM

For many people, escaping materialism is the best way to find happiness. Once you stop assigning value to the objects, activities, and even people in your life according to how much they cost, increased happiness naturally follows.

Stop Making Shopping a Recreational Activity

Stop thinking of the mall as an entertainment venue. Happiness isn't in things. It's within us. The problem with seeing the mall as an entertainment venue is that the place was built on the ideology of materialism. Everything there is for sale. Store owners will do almost anything to get you to buy. And advertising is everywhere. If you define yourself as a "mall shopper," pretty soon you'll feel like you haven't done your duty unless you leave the place with a bag full of stuff you don't need. That's when they have you!

- Don't go to the mall with friends. Go alone, and make it a business trip.

- Know exactly what you want before you go to the store, buy it, and leave the premises immediately.

- Use a thirty-day list. If you decide you really want to buy something, put it on a list. Now tell yourself you cannot buy that item for thirty days. When the thirty days have passed, if you still want the item, go to the store and buy it. This waiting period can help you determine whether or not you want or need the item.

- Remember that happiness comprises two elements. One is the momentary emotion of joy, and the other is the satisfaction derived from living a meaningful life. So, it's essential to work on both aspects.

Buy Used

When you get the urge to buy something, try finding it used instead of new. Buying used gets you out of the mall and into another world. Thrift shops, used-clothing stores, and flea markets operate under a different market sensibility. It's not quite anti-materialistic, but it's certainly less materialistic than the mall sensibility.

- Internet services such as *Craigslist* and *e-Bay* make buying used items much easier than before. The direct exchange such services provide can get you out of the cycle of extreme consumerism.

- Buying used at thrift stores and flea markets usually means you are dealing with another human being, face-to-face, instead of dealing with a faceless corporation.

Limit Television

You don't need to become a television basher; just recognize that TV is dominated by the concerns of advertisers. It's not just that a higher and higher percentage of TV content is ads but that even non-advertising content carries the messages and materialistic ideology of advertisers. The actors who play people in sitcoms, for example, don't wear clothing that they pick out themselves. They wear clothing that fits advertising demographics.

- Force yourself to shut down all TV viewing for one week as an experiment, and if you can't handle this, shut it down for three days.

- Figure out how many hours of TV you watch per week. Then determines what you would truly miss if you cut out TV viewing altogether. Watch only the shows you would truly miss and forget about the rest.

- Watch TV only with other people, never alone. Figuring TV as a communal activity can reduce some of its materialistic overtones as you interact with your fellow viewers instead of sitting inert and allowing yourself to be bombarded by endless ads.

Limit Web Browsing

Unfortunately, the Internet is second only to television for spreading a materialistic ideology. The prevalence of the celebrity culture, incredibility intrusive advertising, and, of course, online shopping make it hard to avoid the rampant materialism.

- Even more than TV, Internet use encourages self-absorption and a solitary lifestyle. Instead of becoming a hermit, participate in *real* social networking—making new, non-virtual, friends—rather than participating in Facebook and Twitter.

- Cut out one Internet function. Most people use the Internet for more than one function. They use it to play games. They use it for getting news. Or, they use it for buying stuff. Cutting out one of these functions is easier than cutting them all out, and it can help you get a handle on your overall Internet usage.

Become More Environmentally Conscious

Thinking green isn't compatible with thinking "stuff," so go green! Most of the serious environmental problems facing us today—including climate change, ever-expanding garbage dumps, and air pollution, to name only a few—have been caused by attempting to buy and sell natural processes.

- Recognize the connection between environmental degradation and a materialistic way of life. For example, buying bottled water produces millions of plastic bottles that end up bobbing up and down in rivers and lakes, not to mention the oceans.

- Make recycling your religion. If you make recycling a way of life, you'll see how foolish it is to assign value to objects based on how much they cost.

- Human beings are part of nature, too. Going green can help you reconstitute your identity.

Declutter

Go through your closets and other storage areas, and start getting rid of stuff you don't use or want anymore. Most people find it a revelation to discover how much rubbish they accumulate over a period of years. Decluttering is a gratifying process and helps you realize how costly mindless consumerism can be. You don't need any of this stuff! You don't enjoy having it. But what you will enjoy is a less cluttered house or apartment.

Participate in non-material forms of entertainment. The world provides many interesting activities that aren't at all related to TV viewing or Internet browsing. Try playing board games, creating art, or hiking. Try visiting relatives and other loved ones more often. Try volunteering with a charity.

Read a book instead of a magazine. Magazines stopped making their profit from subscription fees and store purchases a long time ago. It's all advertising now! Reading a book can provide a respite from being bombarded by magazine ads.

Get to Know Your Neighbors

Get to know them in the way your parents and grandparents used to know them—that is, actually spend some time with them. Have lunch with them; have dinner with them. Find out what bothers them about your neighborhood and what they really like about it. You can nurture positive emotions by practicing appreciation and gratitude.

- Attend non-professional sporting events. Attending professional sports events has become so expensive as to exclude a large part of the working population, especially families. For a family of four to attend a professional baseball game, for example, you can expect to spend as much as $400 or more when you consider tickets, food, souvenirs, and parking: Alternatively, many communities have nearby colleges that play high-quality baseball, and attendance is usually free. The point is to enjoy the game itself, and what does the game have to do with $12.00 cups of beer? For that matter, what's wrong with attending a Little League game and watching twelve-year-olds play out of the love of participation?

- Learn that everything in life has to go once your attachment, be it of value or emotions, to an object can make it a part of your life. And concentrating on these things, you forget to enjoy yourself. So, live happily; don't make any kind of greedy, emotional, or valued attachment to anything. Pursuing meaningful goals helps to improve your life and makes you happy.

UNDERSTANDING THE PSYCHOLOGY AND EFFECTS OF MATERIALISM

It is undeniable that materialism has become a widespread trend in our culture. Just look at the growing desire to make more money and own material goods, and you'll see that there's a rat race to own and enjoy the material world like never before. While possessing worldly possessions and enjoying the materialistic world isn't a terrible habit, it is unquestionably wrong to go to any lengths to forsake moral ideals in the pursuit of material riches.

The Psychology of Materialism

Many folks are obsessed with materialism. Put simply, people are mad after money and money matters. They have a craving for money just like a binge eater who is always searching for food to eat, not knowing that overeating is actually harmful to their overall health. In the same way, materialistic people fail to realize that wasting valuable time only on making money and buying short-lived worldly items will in no sense bring real happiness. Still, people are in haste to own as many material goods as possible. However, there are many negative effects of materialism. Some of them are outlined below.

Effects of the Psychology of Materialism

No Moral Values

People who give importance to money and other worldly things give up moral values to earn worldly possessions. They believe that there is nothing wrong in resorting to selfish acts in order to enjoy the luxuries of life. In fact, some individuals will go to almost any extent to relish the luxuries of worldly life. People often rob and ditch others to make money by amoral means to live a luxuriant life. In the process, most of them murder the very basic values of human life.

Spoiled Relationship

When moral values are kept aside, it greatly impacts your relationship. Whether it's a family relationship or social relationship, people behave like animals when it comes to enjoying worldly lust. Most of them think that there is no hereafter where they will be questioned about their deeds. As a result, they place little importance on close relationships and only pursue monetary affairs.

Unethical Living

Folks with the psychology of materialism often compete with others to gain more materialistic joys. They don't bother whether they're making money through right or wrong means. They are only concerned about how much money they are making in the shortest possible time. Ethical living is no longer given a priority; the only priority is worldly gains. All unethical ways are employed to generate money to live a lavish life.

Final Words

Thus, the psychology of materialism has a lot of negative effects on a person's life. In spite of this, more and more people are running after money and materialism. However, you can avoid becoming a victim of materialism and save yourself from all negative aspects by practicing moral values. If you follow moral values and strive hard in the material world, you will definitely progress like others while maintaining a harmonious relationship with everyone in the society.

COSTLY CONSEQUENCES OF A MATERIALISTIC MINDSET

You may believe that if you work hard enough, you deserve anything you want. Yet, a materialistic mindset comes with a hefty pricetag. The fact that you want to acquire particular items does not make you a materialist. Furthermore, a materialistic mindset doesn't necessitate a large sum of money. However, you may be suffering with materialism if your major concentration is on purchasing and obtaining things to the point that other aspects of life are put aside. A materialistic mindset might have seven potentially severe effects.

You're Never Content

Lack of contentment is one of several costly consequences of a materialistic mindset. Materialistic individuals typically have an obsession with acquiring bigger, better things. They work hard to buy things, but the excitement quickly wears off, and they're on to the next big thing. This creates a dangerous cycle, and unfortunately, these people constantly strive after the wind and never achieve real satisfaction.

False Sense of Success

If you have a materialistic mindset, you might have a warped view of success. Oftentimes, materialistic people base success on the size of a bank account. However, money isn't the definition of success. Additionally, these individuals may view people with less money and fewer possessions as inferior— even if these people live a simple life by choice.

You Might Have Greater Debts

In your quest to always buy the latest new item, regardless of its cost, you run the risk of accumulating massive debt. Some materialistic people don't have a lot of money. Because they're determined to acquire stuff and present a certain image, they may use credit cards on a regular basis. Unfortunately, they don't always have resources to pay off this debt.

You Might Sacrifice Your Savings Account

Money experts recommend saving 10 percent of pay for a rainy day. But if you're materialistic and always buying things to feel better about yourself, most of your disposable income will likely be spent on things you don't really need, such as clothes, jewelry, electronics and vacations. This often results in zero emergency funds, which makes it harder to deal with unexpected expenses.

Avarice

Money is for a protection, and we all need resources to put a roof over our head and food on the table. But if you have a materialistic mindset, you may develop a love of money. And when you love money, it can become your god. You might make irrational decisions and take unnecessary risks in order to acquire more money.

You Buy Things Just Because

Your obsession with buying the latest things might trigger a habit of purchasing stuff just because. And unfortunately, you can accumulate a lot of stuff you don't need, or really want. If you're not careful, materialism can give birth to a spending addiction.

Money Doesn't Buy Happiness

Some people become materialistic because they wrongly believe stuff will make them happier. Although there's some truth behind retail therapy, this form of happiness is often short-lived. Rather then shop and acquire stuff to fill a void, get to the root of the problem and figure out why you're feeling empty inside.

Materialism is a dangerous problem that can advance if left unchecked. It can result in massive debt, deplete your saving,s and trigger a shopping addiction. What other consequences of materialism have you observed?

Materialism

BASIC MINDFULNESS FOSTERS RECOVERY FROM ADDICTION

Simply put, mindfulness is the discipline of becoming more aware of oneself. It is based on ancient trans-Himalayan philosophies of contemplation and awareness cultivation. Even without engaging in meditation, research has shown that the repeated practice of mindfulness activities results in significant changes in traits, forming a predisposition to be more attentive in everyday life. Although mindfulness-based treatment programs are a novel approach to recovery, there is a growing body of evidence to supports its effectiveness.

Misconceptions of Mindfulness

The point of practicing mindfulness isn't to reach a blank mental state. On the contrary, it's about being more aware—more fully present. It's about sharpening one's awareness of moments and thoughts and emotions and sensations. The point is to embrace awareness, not expel awareness from the mind. It's an exercise in curiosity about all that passes through the consciousness, and in freeing the mind from judgment about any of it.

Although mindfulness is a part of various forms of meditation, the two are not the same thing. Meditation is a dedicated activity, planned and executed, whereas mindfulness is best understood as a developed way of thinking about your thoughts and experiences as they are occurring. It's a practice of observing and accepting one's own perceptions of reality in everyday life.

THE ROLE OF MINDFULNESS IN RECOVERY

In recovery, mindfulness allows patients to focus on the present, rather than the past or future. This is especially useful when is it comes to dealing with cravings or unwanted thoughts about substances. Rather than avoid the feelings or emotions that come with those cravings, mindfulness teaches people to name and tolerate their feelings. It allows them to take a non-judgmental approach to their habits or behaviors. The practice of mindfulness gives people an insight into how to deal with negative emotions and situations by allowing compassionate reflection rather than reaching for a substance. If a patient is invited to a small gathering of peers and they know there is going to be an alcohol or an illegal substance there, they may begin to experience stress. They may wonder if they will drink, or they may worry that if their peers pressure them, they will cave. How will it make them look to turn something down? With mindfulness, people can recognize those thoughts as fictitious scenarios. They can deal with these thoughts appropriately.

This is a moment when people realize they have a choice. They don't have to cave to peer pressure; they can choose not to drink. It may help them cope with the realization they have to change their peer group as well. Mindfulness provides the tools needed to be aware of environmental triggers and how to avoid them. Practicing mindfulness also helps in coping with psychological issues that may have influenced substance abuse or developed during recovery. Researchers have used MRI scans to monitor the brain's reaction to mindfulness exercises. According to the scans, the grey matter in the region of the brain known for its role in stress—the amygdala—can become smaller after the exercises are performed. The reduction of stress is important in a patient's motivation for recovery. Ultimately, mindfulness gives those in treatment the tools to properly deal with their emotions and stressors without self-medicating.

EVIDENCE IN SUPPORT OF MINDFULNESS-BASED ADDICTION TREATMENT

Because mindfulness-based relapse prevention (MBRP) is an emerging practice, there has been a rush by researchers to test its efficacy. While an overwhelming amount of evidence points toward a decrease in relapse rates, some evidence points to it being a selective treatment—something that isn't one-size-fits-all. A healthcare provider will know how to make the best decisions and provide effective options. Thus, mindfulness exercises should be applied with discretion. A 2013 study found that those exposed to MBRP showed significantly lower rates of substance use and greater decreases in craving following treatment. Using MRI imaging data, research suggests that MBRP may change neural responses to the experiences of craving and other negative effects, which may reduce the risk of relapse. Other research shows evidence that mindfulness fosters a feeling of acceptance and non-judgment towards a person's addiction. Some studies find that the continued practice of mindfulness gives people an improved ability to recognize and address issues that influence their well-being such as mental illness or trauma. This type of introspective tool supports long-term outcomes. A recently published paper suggests that the type of treatment that works for a patient may be influenced by their disposition. If a person already approaches their behaviors and tendencies with awareness, non-judgment, and acceptance, then they will be more successful in mindfulness-based treatment. However, mindfulness can be learned. Someone without that disposition will likely need a lengthier, more vigorous treatment. Also, what is going on psychologically with a person will determine the efficacy of mindfulness-based treatment. Is there trauma that needs to be addressed? Some mood disorders make concentration and self-awareness more tedious for some than others. Anxiety is a disorder that can shatter a person's concentration. It's vital that patients are being treated for these issues in order to ensure the best outcome with mindfulness-based treatment.

Is There Any Evidence that Mindfulness Works when Battling Addiction?

The short answer is yes. For example, a study funded by the National Institute on Drug Abuse (NIDA) in 2018 found that a mindful awareness training program led to increased positive outcomes for women in addiction treatment. During the study, women learned to identify and perceive internal signals related to their emotions. This helped them to regulate their reactions to various emotions and be kinder to themselves in a healthy way when emotions were triggered.

Mounting evidence suggests that mindfulness can increase addiction recovery odds by strengthening basic positive cognitive processes. Mindfulness-based interventions may be clinically beneficial for treating a variety of substance use disorders, including addictions to alcohol, nicotine, cocaine, and prescription opioids.

With the help of addiction neuroscience, many treatment providers and medical practitioners are turning to the ancient practice of mindfulness to address unhealthy behaviors associated with substance abuse. Some mindfulness-based practices that have recently been integrated into recovery programs include:

- Mindfulness-based stress reduction
- Mindfulness-based cognitive therapy
- Mindfulness-based relapse prevention
- Mindfulness-oriented recovery enhancement

Combining the ancient practice of meditation with modern therapy may be the best line of action for many people going through a complex, life-changing journey of addiction recovery. Cognitive control can be regained, and improved habits can lead to long-term recovery by learning about and practicing mindfulness-based activities.

How Can Mindfulness Help Addiction?

We all have desires, but what takes desire that extra step into addiction? Addiction can be described as a disease of the brain that is defined by cycles of compulsive substance use. An addict's behavior is characterized by limited control over their actions, intense cravings, and continued destructive conduct despite harmful consequences.

Regular mindful practices like meditation or yoga can help cultivate a sense of clarity. This clarity facilitates informed decision-making and serves as the basis for noticeable changes in everyday life. Training in mindfulness increases attention and clarity, making it possible to actively monitor thoughts, emotions, and sensations without allowing them to develop into uncontrollable cravings.

Because mindfulness fosters non-judgmental awareness of habits that are usually given free rein—like cracking open a beer after a day's work, heading for that poker game, or seeing a doctor for an unnecessary prescription—it teaches us that we have choices. What's more, for people in recovery, mindfulness directly exercises the underlying neurological functioning associated with resisting addiction and can help prevent relapse. In addition, mindfulness has been shown to refine executive functioning by providing a higher degree of cognitive control. What this all adds up to is that mindfulness-based practices improve memory, attention, response inhibition, and decision-making.

Mindfulness-Based Cognitive Therapy (MBCT), in particular, has been shown to help prevent relapse. When a person who has struggled with addiction finds the right therapeutic path, the recovery that once seemed like a pipe dream finally becomes attainable.

Why Is Mindfulness Hard to Achieve?

Today's social and professional atmosphere can seem like immersion in a state of rapid and constant change. The persistent high energy and sense of perpetual rushing can cause a sense of disequilibrium, often leading to anxiety and even consequences of mental and emotional overload. The relentless daily exposure to it all can be a lot to manage; keeping a sense of balance, peace, and contentment isn't easy.

Self-therapeutic focus on building a richer and more objective awareness of one's self and world (mindfulness), along with cultivating a mindset of gratitude involves adopting new ways of thinking. Observing our thoughts and ways of processing our experiences require slowing down enough to experience the present more fully.

That can feel awkward for people who have recently come to practice mindfulness. Like any other skill, it takes practice to master it, and every individual must try some techniques to discover which ones are most effective for them. Fortunately, it's fun to do, so its soothing just to keep trying to exercise our own techniques for mindful self-observation.

Even better, there's no possibility of failure while you're trying to be mindful. In efforts at mindfulness, trying is succeeding. In other words, to try to focus on being mindful is what it is to be mindful in that moment.

Mindfulness for Help in Trauma Recovery

Moving through life at high speed is a manner of coping for many people struggling with the effects of past trauma, and practicing mindfulness offers an important tool for helping overcome the often long-lasting effects of trauma. Each person can choose a level of practice to imbue daily consciousness with greater mindfulness.

In making the effort toward more mindful living, a person can anticipate finding their own comfortable pace of the practice. It can be as easy as closing your eyes and/or sitting quietly and intentionally listening to your own thoughts and feelings, without judging them as they flow through you.

Being mindful is being fully present in your environment, being fully aware of your mental, emotional, and physical responses to it, and discovering that you're feeling comfortable with yourself.

How Can I Practice Mindfulness?
Practicing mindfulness is a very simple matter of quieting the mind and paying attention to your thoughts as they flow into and out of your mind. It's a matter of observing your thoughts as they come and go. This is what it is to be present, also known as to live in the moment. It's a way to inner balance and greater happiness.

Of course, being simple doesn't mean it's easy. It does take practice to eventually find oneself more automatically maintaining an ongoing state of mindfulness. So, practice for a few minutes each day, until you find it becoming a more frequent habit. Strengthen your newly-developing habit by continuing to practice it intentionally during times when you find you have drifted out of the mindset.

Continue this process until you find yourself eventually living more continuously in a mindful state. But do recall that mindfulness is an endeavor that offers progress to those who continue the practice—not a permanent accomplishment. Take comfort in that fact as you embark on an ever-aspiring life-long journey of gently coaxing your mind into greater extents of mindful awareness.

External Aids for Cultivating Mindfulness
Practicing mindfulness can be challenging in our busy lives and fast-paced environment, but we have the benefit of a great wealth of resources for cultivating mindfulness. If it helps, you might try attending organized mindfulness group sessions. There are also abundant group meditation opportunities. Alternatively, just walk, sit, lie down, bike, or do something else that helps you free your consciousness to use the activity for focusing your awareness on all the thoughts and sensations you experience while engaged in it.

Modern technologies offer additional resources for developing mindfulness. For example, you can watch online instructional videos and podcasts offering mindfulness guidance. There are even free apps to aid in meditation, and others for developing and practicing mindfulness.

PRACTICING MINDFULNESS CAN STRENGTHEN ADDICTION RECOVERY

Mindfulness is about learning to be present in the moment and aware of your surroundings. It's an old Buddhist practice that's been scientifically verified. Every year, new research confirms the advantages of practicing mindfulness meditation on a regular basis. Mindfulness can be particularly beneficial in the fight against addiction. Mindfulness-based stress reduction (MBSR), mindfulness-based cognitive therapy (MBCT), and dialectical behavioral therapy (DBT) are just a few of the therapeutic modalities that have previously included it. Adding mindfulness practice to your recovery can help in a variety of ways, including the ones listed below.

Mindfulness Is the Opposite of Avoidance

Substance uses disorders often begin as a means of avoiding painful emotions, intrusive thoughts, social anxiety, and physical pain. What begins as a palliative or a crutch soon turns into addiction. When you practice mindfulness, you train yourself to accept whatever you're experiencing rather than trying to escape it. By accepting what's happening and investigating the experience, you learn that unpleasant experiences are temporary and tolerable.

Mindfulness Helps You Learn to Relax

Learning to relax is a crucial skill in addiction recovery. It helps reduce stress, which also helps reduce pain, anxiety, cravings, and the physical harm associated with chronic stress. Most of us aren't aware when we are becoming stressed because it creeps in gradually. Before we know it, we're tense and irritable. Practicing mindfulness every day has two major benefits for stress. First, it's a daily break during which you can sit quietly and intentionally relax. This prevents stress from perpetually accumulating. Second, you become more aware of what's going on in your body and mind and you take a moment to relax when you become aware of the tension creeping in.

Knowing how to relax is an essential skill for managing anxiety and cravings.

Mindfulness Reduces the Recurrence of Depression

At least half of people who seek treatment for a substance-use disorder also have a co-occurring mental health issue. The most common of these mental health issues are depression and anxiety disorders. About 17 percent of depressed people will develop an alcohol-use disorder at some point, and about 18 percent will develop a drug use disorder. A review in JAMA Internal Medicine of forty-seven studies on mindfulness meditation found that the practice relieved symptoms of depression to a degree comparable to medication and that it also improved symptoms of pain and anxiety. Other studies have found that mindfulness can reduce the risk of recurrence of major depression. As many as 80 percent of people who have an episode of major depression will have a relapse. Mindfulness-based cognitive therapy has been shown to reduce the risk of relapse by 43 percent. For many people recovering from a substance use disorder, a significant reduction in depression risk can make a huge difference.

Mindfulness Lets You Respond Instead of React

One reason addiction is so hard to beat is that it's a pattern of conditioned responses. The part of your brain responsible for higher reasoning essentially gets cut out of the decision-making process, and you react reflexively to stimuli associated with drugs and alcohol. Practicing mindfulness gradually undoes this conditioning. One imaging study of expert meditators found that mindfulness meditation actually changes the structure of the brain. The prefrontal cortex—the region responsible for attention, self-control, planning, and working memory, among other things—becomes thicker and more connected to other areas of the brain. And the amygdala—a part of the brain involved with emotional responses, especially identifying threats and initiating the "fight or flight" response—becomes smaller. In other words, when you practice mindfulness meditation, you feel less threatened by things in general, and you're better able to think things through.

You also learn to identify less with your own thoughts. We often fall into the trap of thinking something is true just because we think it. If you're in the habit of thinking negative or self-critical thoughts, believing those thoughts can lead to depression or anxiety. Mindfulness practice can help you see your thoughts—both good and bad—for what they are, essentially guesses, rather than iron truths about the world. Then, you can begin to challenge or ignore thoughts that work against you.

Mindfulness Encourages Compassion

Compassion is important in addiction recovery for two main reasons. First, it helps you connect with other people, especially other people recovering from addiction. Having a strong social support system and feeling a sense of belonging is one of the best predictors of a successful recovery. However, this support can be challenging to build, as many people who are newly sober often feel isolated and ashamed. One might think someone in treatment would easily identify with others in treatment, since they have so much in common. Still, paradoxically, many people are critical and judgmental of others, often taking the attitude of "I'm not like the other people here." Cultivating an attitude of compassion can help you see that you're all really in the same boat. Practicing mindfulness can encourage those feelings of compassion by allowing you to see your own situation more clearly and become less protective of your own self-image.

The second way compassion helps you recover from addiction is that you are able to extend compassion to yourself. People in recovery often feel a deep sense of shame or guilt and even feel like they don't deserve to be happy. Being able to feel compassion for yourself allows you to move forward. Having compassion for yourself also improves the way is you talk to yourself: You become less self-critical and judgmental, which reduces your feelings of depression, anxiety, and negativity.

MINDFULNESS AND MEDITATION FOR RECOVERY

If you use a substance on a regular basis, your brain will undoubtedly undergo changes that lead to addiction. To rewire an addicted brain, you must go through a treatment program that heals both the body and the brain. It's a huge accomplishment to achieve abstinence. However, you will continue to suffer when you encounter triggering situations in your life. Fortunately, there is a technique that might assist you in avoiding such triggers. Meditation is the name for this technique.

What Is Meditation?
Meditation is used in outpatient rehab centers but can also be used by anyone at home for the same purpose—the goal is to foster well-being.

There are many meditation techniques, but the clients of outpatient drug rehab centers are taught the techniques that are within beginners' capabilities. Here are the most popular and effective options.

Mindfulness Meditation

Though this technique is one of the simplest, it's still very effective. The goal is to reinforce your awareness and observe your thoughts and sensations—to do the things addicted people often don't do. Here's how you can practice it:

- Sit up straight. Your spine, neck, and head should be in one line. Put your hands where they're comfortable (if you've tried yoga or stretching, you may feel comfortable in the traditional cross-legged posture).

- Close your eyes.

- Sit quietly and still. Allow your thoughts and sensations to wander in and out of the body without labeling them as good or bad.

- You can open your eyes if you want. But you should direct them a few feet in front of the body, fixing your gaze on a fixed object on the ground.

- If you stop focusing on your thoughts and concentrate on your breath or a specific object, you are doing everything right. Now you can proceed to the following technique.

Breathing Meditation

The purpose of breathing meditation is to calm the mind and develop inner peace. It's easy to practice:

- Sit in the same position that you used for the first technique and close your eyes.

- Concentrate on your breath. Inhale deeply and exhale slowly.

- Relax your muscles. Take the energy your brain spends on thinking about your cravings and divert it toward your body.

- Pay careful attention to breathing. Feel how air is coming in and out through your nostrils.

- If some thoughts start to distract you, return to your breathing.

Water Meditation

This technique isn't usually included in outpatient rehab programs. But you should try it at home. It's an effective way to deal with the burden of your old drug-related thoughts. Make sure you have enough time before you dive in!

- Run a warm bath.

- It's a good idea to mix it with aromatherapy, and light aroma candles or add bath salts or oils.

- Turn off the tap, but allow for small drips of warm water to continue dripping into the tub.

- Plant yourself in the bath in a comfortable position.

- Focus on breathing as described in the above technique.

- If your mind gets distracted, return the focus to the sound of the dripping water.

Moving Meditation

People usually meditate while sitting still. But the Buddha himself recommended meditating while moving. This technique is aimed at immersing in the world of nature, which implies an absence of thought and a sense of unity with nature. Here's how to practice it:

- Find a perfect place for this technique: a garden, forest, lake, river, or other natural surrounding near your house.

- You can walk, run, or ride a bicycle. The emphasis is not on your motion but a state of mind. If you choose walking or running, keep your focus on your feet hitting the ground. If you're cycling, focus on your feet pushing the pedals.

- With every step you take, imagine how negative energy is leaving and positive energy takes up vacant space.

- Pay attention to the processes in your body—the contraction and relaxation of the muscles, the air coming in and out, the blood coursing through your veins.

- The length of a meditation session depends on the time you need to feel fulfillment. Usually, 10–15 minutes is enough.

BENEFITS OF MINDFULNESS AND MEDITATION FOR RECOVERY

It's estimated that meditation and mindfulness practices have existed for over five thousand years. Most people think of meditation as a person sitting in a quiet place with their legs crossed, arms out, and fingers pointed towards the sky, while either humming or sitting entirely in silence.

There is much more to meditation than a person's location and body position, however.

From calming the mind to healing the body, meditation and mindfulness work together to change the brain and the body. If a person starts meditation in January and practices it daily, by June they may have a completely different brain—neurologically speaking, that is.

Meditation and mindfulness go hand in hand. Without one or the other, there is little to no chance that the brain will receive the full benefits of either one.

The benefits of meditation and mindfulness are almost too numerous to count and will impact each person differently. We do know for sure that those who practice them regularly for an extended period of time tend to foster more compassion, empathy, and love for themselves and others, while boosting memory and focus.

These benefits are helpful throughout day-to-day life and help improve one's mood and relationships with others.

In addition, mediation and mindfulness also provide these important benefits:

- Lowered heart rate and blood pressure
- Decreased stress, anxiety, and depression
- Improved work and school performance
- Reduction in work burnout
- Enhanced overall health and immunity
- Improvements related to various forms of recovery

Many of these benefits are due to the calm mental state and changes in the brain that meditation and mindfulness provide for those who practice it regularly.

How Do Meditation and Mindfulness Change the Brain?
Neuroplasticity is the ability of the brain to adapt and change over time, either positively or negatively.

When a person commits to a specific practice repeatedly, the neural pathways in the brain adapt to this repetition and accommodate for the new sensory input. Part of this is the brain's way of becoming more efficient by creating a habit loop that automates repetitive tasks so the person doesn't have to think about the action(s) at all.

The brain essentially wires new pathways to work in conjunction with one another. Neuroplasticity and changes in the brain are ongoing. If a person wants to reverse changes that have occurred, neuroplasticity can accommodate that, too.

Meditation and mindfulness play an important role in increasing the thickness of the brain's cortex, which is vital for cognitive function, attention, and sensory processing.

At the same time, long-term meditation has been shown to increase the density of grey matter in the brain to improve cardiovascular function, learning, and memory.

Additionally, mindfulness can improve brain connections, awareness, and emotional regulation.

Both meditation and mindfulness provide many positive changes in the brain, and the more a person practices them, the more pronounced the changes will be over time.

Meditation and mindfulness have shown great promise for those in recovery from physical and mental health issues such as stroke, traumatic brain injury, addiction, depression, and other mental illnesses.

Many of these health issues negatively change the brain's wiring, and these changes override the brain's normal functioning. But as mentioned earlier, the brain is neuroplastic, so whatever changes occur can be changed through practice and perseverance.

In the sense of traumatic brain injury, these are usually physical changes that are detrimental to the brain's circuitry.

For those with an addiction to drugs or alcohol, the addictive substances change the function and structure of the brain, which after becoming addicted, relies on the drugs or alcohol to take the place of neurotransmitters like serotonin and dopamine.

Regular and extended mediation and mindfulness practice can help the brain return to normal functioning for those in many types of recovery.

And because they promote focus and help calm the mind, the brain becomes more efficient at handling routine tasks while improving mood, relationships, and a positive outlook on life.

REAL-LIFE STORY ABOUT MINDFULNESS
(a client of mine)

I have dreadful memories from my childhood of feeling frightened and anxious about sundry aspects of life. Going to sleep was the worst.

Ideally, I would have liked to stay at my mother's side day and night.

I didn't want to go to school because I was scared of being in a big group of children I don't know why, but I didn't want to be in a car with more than three people in either, as I was feeling terribly anxious about the car breaking.

I didn't want to be on a boat for fear it would sink. I didn't want to be at home with a babysitter because I was worried that my mother wasn't coming back.

Many things terrified me

I constantly believed that something bad was going to happen to me—that I would get lost, that I had to go to hospital, that I was going to be separated from my mother and sister, that I was going to be in a lot of pain, that I was going to die . . .

Those were some of my catastrophic thoughts that kept me in a constant state of high alert and worry.

Life felt very scary to me, and my anxiety prevented me from experiencing untold joy.

Of course, I had therapy when I was a child, and this continued throughout my academic career and into young adulthood. It reduced the level of anxiety I was suffering from considerably.

Still, anxiety was a constant unpleasant companion in my life for almost four decades until I was introduced to the practice of mindfulness in 2008 (when I was forty).

Thanks to mindfulness, I was able to understand myself better, including the underlying cause of my anxiety.

That in itself isn't a remedy, but it helped me bring understanding and compassion to myself, and that's helped me to come into a different, more supportive relationship with myself.

My parents divorced when my sister and I were two and three years old respectively. My mother never remarried and brought us up a single mum who needed to work full-time.

It meant that we had to grow up quickly, and that felt deeply unsettling and unsafe. Don't get me wrong; my mother didn't do anything wrong; this isn't about blaming my parents. It's just that she wasn't around enough to reassure me that I was okay.

Mindfulness *Has* Helped Me Become M*ore* Aware *of* My Stress Pattern

When I feel anxious and then stressed, I have a narrative in my head that goes like this: *It's too much; I have too much work to do; I can't cope; I won't be able to do it.* These thoughts trigger my mind's alarm system, which in turn triggers more tension in my body and makes my breath shallow and inhibited, which impacts the choices I make; what I say to my colleagues, friends, partner, family, etc.; and how I say it (a.k.a. knee-jerk reactions).

Anxiety—worrying about what hasn't yet happened—has inhibited me from fully living.

Then, to top it all off, I beat myself up for being so stressed, inefficient, grumpy or moody, which adds another layer of anxiety and stress. And this is the crucial bit that was a complete eye-opener for me: harsh self-criticism or self-judgement is the very thing that puts the most pressure on me (on us), creating the most stress and anxiety, leading to depression.

The Practice of Mindfulness Has Helped Me to See Things for What They Are

Yes, I have work to do, and deadlines that perhaps are unpleasant, but they're just deadlines, and work is just work, and giving a talk is just giving a talk—no more no less. It's called primary experience. What we do with it (i.e., how we interpret what happens to us) is called secondary experience, and that's what can cause us a lot of pain, depending on how we interpret, judge, and analyse life's events.

Mindfulness isn't an idea; it's a practice—one that requires daily commitment, faith, and stamina.

So, when I feel stressed or anxious, I now notice my breath getting shallow, I recognize the thoughts racing through my head and the feelings in my body (e.g., tightness, racing heart, anxiety, sweating, panic, overwhelm), and take deeper breaths and let my breath find its natural rhythm again, which allows my mind and body to calm down and relax.

Mindfulness Has Transformed How I Experience Myself

It has helped me see and understand my helpful and unhelpful habitual ways of thinking and behaving, which in turn has helped me respond differently—more kindly and compassionately—to myself, others, and life's challenges.

Today, I still suffer from anxiety occasionally, particularly in the early hours of the morning when I wake up with sweaty sheets and a racing heart. The difference is that today I know what I need to do.

I expand my in-breath and slow down my out-breath. I feel my body on the mattress—my feet, legs, bum, back, and the back of my head. I become aware of whatever catastrophic thought is going through my mind, then ask myself: is this true? 99 percent of the time, the answer is "no." I'm back in the here and now and continue to sleep.

Mindfulness is not an idea; it's a practice. It requires daily commitment, faith and stamina. The pay-off is huge and can be life-changing. It's certainly given me back *my* life!

HYPNOTHERAPY IN ADDICTION TREATMENT

Hypnotherapy is a research-based addiction treatment that may also be used to treat a variety of other psychological issues. Hypnotherapy is a psychological treatment that combines hypnosis and psychotherapy. Hypnotherapy is provided by a skilled therapist, usually a certified psychologist, to a client who has been told about, understands, and consents to the treatment.

Hypnosis is a type of trance induction in which one person—the hypnotist or hypnotherapist—induces an altered state of consciousness in another person or group of people— the hypnotic patient or subjects. The shift in awareness that happens during hypnosis is more than a sensation; it can be measured and monitored using EEG readings from hypnotized individuals' brains. The person is more open to suggestion when in a state of hypnosis.

The practice of inducing hypnosis in oneself is known as self-hypnosis (or auto-hypnosis). The primary difference between guided and self-hypnosis is that self-hypnosis necessitates knowledge of how to induce hypnosis in yourself.

HOW HYPNOTHERAPY HELPS WITH ADDICTION

While in a hypnotic trance, the person being hypnotized, or hypnotic subject, is more open to suggestion by the hypnotist or hypnotherapist. They generally become more passive and compliant with suggestions as directed by the hypnotist or hypnotherapist. Under hypnosis, people can become more imaginative, more open to fantasy, and sometimes, better able to access long-forgotten memories, although these memories aren't always reliable.

This relaxed and suggestible state can help people gain a different perspective on their addictive behaviors. What normally seems impossible—quitting a substance or behavior that is central to one's existence—can seem achievable and desirable.

Though everyone responds differently to hypnosis, many people undergoing hypnotherapy treatments may develop a capacity to break free from certain long-term behavior patterns in the waking state.

There are many myths about hypnosis and hypnotherapy, and many of them raise the issue of whether or not hypnosis is effective or safe. Yet, hypnosis is considered safe when performed by a trained hypnotherapist, and even self-hypnosis is also regarded as safe.

Some studies have shown that hypnotherapy can help with addictions since hypnosis can allow certain people, through the power of suggestion, to strengthen their willpower in overcoming their addictive urges and cravings. The hypnotic state decreases a person's peripheral awareness, heightening attention and suggestibility to potentially effectively alter the neurophysiological networks capable of rewiring certain patterns and conditioning. This means a person's feelings and behaviors continue to be influenced even after they have come out of a hypnotic trance.

However, those who think that hypnosis is somehow magical and will erase their addiction in a single session are likely to be disappointed. Hypnotherapy is a tool to unlock human potential through the power of suggestion; it isn't a magic formula.

Hypnotherapy Isn't an Instant Fix
Hypnosis can help people to address both their addictions and associated problems. Still, these issues are complex and challenging both for the client and for the therapist, and hypnotherapy doesn't work for everyone.

REAL-LIFE STORY
(a client of mine)

There are few things worse than not feeling like yourself due to mental health struggles. Some people will never live through this experience. But the reality is, 20 percent of the population suffers from mental illness. I'm in that 20 percent. There have been three different times in my life when I didn't feel like myself for an extended period: The first time it happened, my grandma had passed away, and I began experiencing OCD symptoms around the age of ten. At that point, therapy ended up helping me break the cycle.

Then, when I was in my second semester as a college sophomore, I fell into a spiral of insomnia, anxiety, OCD, and depression caused by heartbreak. Family financial issues played a part in my turmoil too, and I felt like I was losing the joyful, calm, sleep-loving person I had been. I had disassociated from myself, and all I wanted to be was the person before the trauma.

Luckily, I went into therapy and (at first reluctantly) started on an antidepressant. Then, life struck once again. Last year, I was laid off; around the same time, my uncle passed away. To say my body didn't react well to the financial pressure and heartache is an understatement. I developed PTSD, my insomnia came back with a vengeance, my OCD thoughts were constant, and my anxiety was paralyzing. I began to dread the things I once loved. Dressing up, wearing makeup, going to concerts, writing, and hanging out with friends felt torturous.

When you're desperate enough, you'll do anything to feel like you again. For me that meant trying something I had never before considered: hypnosis.

For people living with OCD, PTSD, phobias, anxiety, or depression, sometimes therapy and medication don't feel like enough. That's where hypnosis comes in. "Anxiety is actually self-hypnosis in a negative way—when you [practice] hypnosis, you reprogram the mind with different beliefs," hypnotherapist and psychotherapist Fayina Cohen says. She adds that the stereotypes about hypnosis being fake or for hippies are just that: *stereotypes.*

But the stigma and skepticism attached to hypnosis mean a lot of people struggling with mental health issues don't know it's a real option for them. My therapist, whom I credit with a ton of my improvements, recommended I try hypnosis. I, of course, reacted like most people: with serious doubts. I imagined someone waving a long, gold chain connected to a pocket watch in front of my face while I miraculously passed out. But when you're barely able to function, you'll try just about anything. That's how I came to try hypnosis—and how I became a believer in its power.

Appointments with my hypnotist began with talk therapy that helped to inform the second part, the hypnosis session itself. My hypnotist read from a carefully crafted script, which she adjusted each week based on the issues we were targeting. The sessions would range from fifteen to thirty minutes, and for about eight months, I had homework: to listen to a recording before I would go to bed.

The recordings themselves don't always make a ton of sense, but embedded in them are commands targeted at your subconscious mind. The commands are meant to bring you into a more relaxed state—akin to what you feel when you daydream or when you miss an exit driving on the highway (something called "highway hypnosis"). "Your subconscious mind is loaded with negative messages, so it's necessary to have a hypnotist clear this stuff out for you," explains certified clinical hypnotist Joanne Ferdman of Theta Healing Arts in Huntington, New York. "Hypnotherapy is great for managing your thoughts, clearing out negative experiences and giving you empowering messages." But while your mind is taking in said thoughts, hypnosis isn't mind control. "Hypnosis isn't something that can make you do something against your will," explains Ferdman. "Your conscious mind already knows what you want to work on. I can't give you a suggestion that your conscious mind isn't in complete agreement with."

When it comes to results, timing is different for everyone. Some people see full changes—including greater relaxation, positivity, and feelings of control—in just a few sessions; others take longer to start to heal. It depends on the person and the state of their subconscious. According to Ferdman, "We have sixty thousand thoughts a day, and most of them are negative." The more negativity you're dealing with, the longer it may take to notice the effect of hypnosis—no matter how much you consciously want things to change.

Essentially, hypnosis is a series of reminders to reduce anxiety and fear, encouraging clients' minds to go in more positive directions when they feel overwhelmed by negativity. Sometimes it's necessary for hypnotists to clear out past experiences, which means they'll do something called "regression"—they'll guide you back to the first time a traumatic experience occurred and help you process it so that you can release it from your subconscious.

If you're still with me, and intrigued, you're not alone. According to hypnotists, hypnosis is becoming a more commonly used practice. "Because of the Internet, there's more education that expels the myth of hypnosis," Cohen says. "In the last ten years, I've been getting more phone calls about hypnosis than ever before."

Here are some things to keep in mind if you're willing to give hypnosis a try:

- Find a hypnotist you trust. Do your research, inquire about their training and certification, and ask to speak to past clients of theirs. Confidence in your care provider, whatever their specialty, is key.

- Focus on your motivation to change. You may not be fully convinced of the potential at first, but if you remain open-minded and stick with it, results will likely follow.

- Hypnosis is a partnership: Both you and your hypnotist work together throughout the healing process. Whether you're listening to your hypnotist read a script or taking in their tapes on repeat, it takes two.

- You don't need to be actively listening for hypnosis to work. The commands and messages your hypnotist embeds in your script are absorbed by the subconscious mind

- You're in control of your session. You still have free will, and you're not in a trance. The hypnotist is just there there to facilitate the hypnotic state.

- You're not too "strong-willed" to be hypnotized. The hypnotist is helping you to hypnotize yourself—you're not giving in or tricking yourself into a state of mind you don't actually want to enter. This is something you're doing for you, as part of a full treatment plan you and your care providers work out together.

Finally, hypnosis wasn't an easy or automatic fix for me. It required patience, commitment, and consistency in showing up to my appointments and listening to my recordings. But I'm so glad I gave hypnosis a chance. I count it as one of the therapeutic techniques that helped me feel like myself again—and that has been worth every minute I've spent on it.

WHAT HYPNOSIS FEELS LIKE DURING HYPNOTHERAPY

In a trance state, a person becomes less aware of what's going on around them, while instead focusing deeply on some aspect of their inner experience. These inner experiences can involve their thoughts, their feelings, their memories, their imagination, and their sensations—especially sensations associated with relaxation.

There are three central aspects of the hypnotic trance. These are absorption, dissociation, and suggestibility.

Absorption is a kind of deep mental focus. The person who is being hypnotized becomes deeply absorbed and mentally involved in whatever they are perceiving, imagining or thinking about. They are concentrating very intently, in much the same way you might become absorbed in a book you are reading or a movie you are watching.

The dissociative aspect of the hypnotic trance means that the person being hypnotized separates the aspects of the hypnotic experience that they are focusing on from other potential distractions that they would usually be aware of at the same time to an unusual degree. For example, the hypnotist might suggest that the person being hypnotized lift their arm.

The person being hypnotized is actually in control of what they are doing, despite the dissociative experience that it might seem that their arm was being controlled by some outside force unknown to them.

Hypnosis is an altered state of consciousness that is sometimes used in hypnotherapy to treat people with addictions. Although hypnotherapy isn't typically the first line of treatment for people with addictions, there are many people who have successfully used it to quit smoking without any other interventions. One study suggested that hypnotherapy was even more effective than nicotine replacement therapy for quitting smoking.

Hypnotherapy may help with other addictions as well, either on its own or in combination with other psychotherapies such as cognitive behavioral therapy. While it doesn't have a large body of research regarding its effectiveness in addictions, there are some studies that support its use. If you have tried other treatments and haven't yet successfully overcome your addiction, hypnotherapy might be worth considering.

HISTORY OF HYPNOSIS

The use of the hypnotic-like trance states dates back thousands of years, but hypnosis began to grow during the late eighteenth century from the work of a physician named Franz Mesmer. The practice got off to a poor start thanks to Mesmer's mystical views, but interest eventually shifted to a more scientific approach.

Hypnotism became more important in the field of psychology in the late nineteenth century and was used by Jean-Martin Charcot to treat women experiencing what was then known as hysteria. This work influenced Sigmund Freud and the development of psychoanalysis.

More recently, there have been a number of different theories to explain exactly how hypnosis works. One of the best-known theories is Hilgard's neo-dissociation theory of hypnosis.

According to Hilgard, people in a hypnotic state experience a split consciousness in which there are two different streams of mental activity. While one stream of consciousness responds to the hypnotist's suggestions, another dissociated stream processes information outside of the hypnotized individual's conscious awareness.

WHAT IS HYPNOSIS?

Like other states of consciousness—such as normal waking consciousness, sleep, dreaming, and intoxication from various drugs—the experience of hypnosis is unique to the person experiencing it. So, although there are features of the hypnotic state that are common among people who are hypnotized, it's never exactly the same from one person to another, nor is it the same each time the same person is hypnotized.

Like all other states, a hypnotic trance is highly affected by set and setting. Set and setting refer to the mindset and environment that a person has during the experience.

Many people are put off trying hypnotherapy because they have seen stage hypnotism or something like it on television and fear that if they are hypnotized, they will lose control, do something embarrassing, or that they will find the experience unpleasant. Most of the time, the opposite is true.

Hypnotherapeutic hypnosis is different from stage hypnosis, which is induced for the entertainment of an audience.

There are some common feelings and thought processes that people tend to experience while undergoing hypnosis for therapeutic purposes. This description isn't going to be an exact fit for every hypnotic subject all of the time, however. If you're considering hypnotherapy, it will give you an idea of what to expect.

Relaxation

Relaxation is a central aspect of hypnosis and involves both mental and physical relaxation. Hypnosis doesn't actually cause relaxation, per se. Rather, the process of hypnotic induction involves you following the hypnotherapist's suggestions that you relax your mind and body.

For example, the hypnotherapist might suggest a feeling of heaviness in one or more parts of your body. Because hypnosis is a collaborative process between the hypnotherapist and client, you might notice a feeling of heaviness in the body part(s) suggested. However, it is actually up to you, not the therapist, to cause relaxation.

Unlike the way that hypnosis is often portrayed, where a hypnotic subject carries out the orders of a hypnotist, the suggestions made by the hypnotherapist are typically communicated as an invitation, not a command. As you think about the suggestions the hypnotherapist makes, you might find yourself thinking something like, *Actually, it would be really nice to relax right now,* then find it quite easy to let go of tension, and relax. There is no "have to" about it.

Intense Focus

Another feature of hypnosis is a particular kind of intense mental focus. As with relaxation, this is entirely under the control of the person being hypnotized, not the therapist.

Because hypnotherapy typically takes place in a private, quiet space, focusing on the words of the therapist is usually quite natural and straightforward. Most people find it easy to let go of distractions and to focus their attention on the topic the hypnotherapist is talking about.

The therapist is trained to guide your thought processes in a particular way that is known to be beneficial in the process of overcoming addictive behavior controlling pain, or helping with a variety of other mental, emotional, and behavioral problems. People under hypnosis will naturally focus on what the therapist is saying.

The therapist will discuss what will happen with clients before beginning hypnotherapy. You will have already discussed with the hypnotherapist the reason you are seeking treatment and what your goals are for therapy.

The therapist will lead the process in a way that allows you to think about your addiction and related problems in a focused way. However, because care is taken to ensure you are relaxed and calm, it isn't usually overwhelming, in the way it can be when you have a lot of conflicting information to process.

Open-Mindedness

One key aspect of hypnosis is to try and create a state of heightened suggestibility. When people engage in counseling for addictive behaviors, they typically think of many reasons why the helpful suggestions of the counselor won't work. It can become a long series of "yes, buts . . ."

When people are under hypnosis, they often become more open to considering possibilities than they are in their normal, wide-awake state. This open-mindedness can, in some people, lead to an increased sense of personal power in which the person realizes they are capable of much more than they previously thought possible.

Again, this open-mindedness shouldn't be confused with a lack of control. Although people under hypnosis might find themselves considering things they wouldn't normally, they don't typically do anything that would violate their value system. Instead, there is a sense of possibilities that weren't apparent before, coupled with a willingness to see things differently.

Sometimes, people realize their problems with addiction are worsened by inflexible modes of thinking that disappear under hypnosis.

Sensory Changes

Hypnosis is well known for its ability to induce unusual sensory experiences, most notably, to allow people to experience sensations such as pain differently from usual. In fact, this effect is so profound that some people have even undergone surgery without an anesthetic. It can also produce differences in the way that visual and auditory sensations are experienced.

As with other aspects of hypnosis, these changes are controlled by the person under hypnosis, not by the hypnotherapist, who is simply offering suggestions. Pain perception, for example, is strongly influenced by the level of anxiety being experienced by the person in pain. In a state of deep relaxation, many people find that without the anxiety present, they are better able to disconnect from pain, which leads to another aspect of hypnosis—detachment.

Detachment

Under hypnosis, some people experience a sense of detachment or dissociation, as if they are slightly removed from what they are experiencing. Some people describe this as observing themselves from outside or as if they're a character on a TV screen. However, people under hypnosis continue to be aware of where they are and what they're doing.

This feeling of detachment can range from feeling involved in the hypnotic process, yet observing it as if from an outside point of view simultaneously, to flipping back and forth between watching from the outside and being involved in the experience. Some people don't get this observer effect at all, whereas, for others; it is very apparent.

People sometimes find that this feeling of detachment can help them see situations more objectively, without being caught up in their usual emotions.

The way people typically describe the feeling of being hypnotized during hypnotherapy is to be in a physical calmness and mental relaxation. In this state, they are able to focus deeply on what they are thinking about. They usually feel open-minded and willing to think about and experience life differently, often in a more detached way than usual.

That said, there is no right way to feel when undergoing hypnosis. If you are curious about trying hypnotherapy as a way of treating addiction, make sure that the person you are working with is qualified to treat you.

For example, your state psychology licensing board should be able to direct you to psychologists who are qualified in hypnotherapy. A range of health professionals can be trained in hypnotherapy including physicians, nurses, and dentists, although it is not usually part of their standard training.

Types of Hypnosis
There are a few different ways that hypnosis can be delivered:

- Guided Hypnosis: This form of hypnosis involves using tools such as recorded instructions and music to induce a hypnotic state. Online sites and mobile apps often utilize this form of hypnosis.

- Hypnotherapy: Hypnotherapy is the use of hypnosis in psychotherapy and is practiced by licensed physicians and psychologists to treat conditions including depression, anxiety, post-traumatic stress disorder (PTSD), and eating disorders.

- Self-Hypnosis: Self-hypnosis is a process that occurs when a person self-induces a hypnotic state. It is often used as a self-help tool for controlling pain or managing stress.

IMPACT OF HYPNOSIS

What impact does hypnosis have? The experience of hypnosis can vary dramatically from one person to another.

Some hypnotized individuals report feeling a sense of detachment or extreme relaxation during the hypnotic state while others even feel that their actions seem to occur outside of their conscious volition. Other individuals may remain fully aware and able to carry out conversations while under hypnosis.

Experiments by researcher Ernest Hilgard demonstrated how hypnosis can be used to dramatically alter perceptions. After instructing a hypnotized individual not to feel pain in their arm, the participant's arm was then placed in ice water. While non-hypnotized individuals had to remove their arm from the water after a few seconds due to the pain, the hypnotized individuals were able to leave their arms in the icy water for several minutes without experiencing pain.

Tips

While many people think that they cannot be hypnotized, research has shown that a large number of people are more hypnotizable than they believe. Research suggests that:

- Between 10% to 15% of people are very responsive to hypnosis.
- Approximately 10% of adults are considered difficult or impossible to hypnotize.
- Children tend to be more susceptible to hypnosis.
- People who can become easily absorbed in fantasies are more responsive to hypnosis.

Suppose you are interested in being hypnotized, it is important to remember to approach the experience with an open mind—people who view hypnosis in a positive light tend to respond better.

If you are interested in trying hypnotherapy, it is important to look for a professional who has credentials and experience in the use of hypnosis as a therapeutic tool.

While there are many places that offer hypnosis training and certification, it may be helpful to look for a mental health professional who has been certified by the American Society of Clinical Hypnosis. Their program is open to health professionals with a master's degree and requires forty hours of approved workshop training, twenty hours of individual training, and two years of practice in clinical hypnosis.

Treating Addiction with Hypnosis

We're currently on an upswing in scientific interest in hypnosis, and a number of studies have found some promising results in using hypnosis to treat addiction. For example, one small study found that treatment that included hypnosis for alcohol use disorder led to an impressive 77 percent sobriety rate after one year. Another small study of people with opioid use disorder found that hypnosis helped all participants remain abstinent from all drugs for six months and 56 percent remained abstinent from heroin for two years. These were small preliminary studies, but they suggest hypnosis may be a useful tool for addiction treatment.

Hypnosis May Enhance the Effect of Other Treatment Methods

In addition to treating addiction directly, hypnosis may be useful in addressing some of the factors that contribute to addiction. These typically include mental health issues (e.g., major depression, anxiety, and bipolar disorder), trauma, and dysfunctional relationships—in addition to genetic factors, which, unfortunately, we're stuck with for the moment. Insofar as hypnosis can help improve these issues, it can help your chances of long-term recovery success too.

Hypnosis Can Help with Mental Health Issues

At least half of people with substance-use issues also have some kind of co-occurring mental health issue. Addiction and mental illness each make the other worse, and they must be treated simultaneously. Hypnosis may be useful in conjunction with other therapeutic methods. As noted above, hypnosis is a skillful way of managing your attention through subtle suggestion and reframing.

In a way, this is what your therapist is trying to accomplish anyway. For example, a therapist using CBT might help you reframe a situation by bringing to your attention your irrational beliefs about the situation. Hypnosis can be used as an extension of this process.

Hypnosis May Help You Manage Pain

Many people develop substance-use issues because they are taking opioids for chronic pain. This puts them in a bind because they're afraid that quitting opioids will leave them defenseless against the pain. However, there are other ways of treating chronic pain, and hypnosis may play a significant part. Pain feels real and undeniable, but it's actually complex and somewhat ephemeral.

It depends to some extent on our expectations and how we think about pain. In this regard, hypnosis can be helpful. As noted above, hypnosis has been used in battlefield medicine, and its use for surgery is pretty well established. If it can help you through surgery, it can help with chronic pain, too. Just relieving some of your distress about pain can make the pain less intense and make it easier to give up your reliance on pain medication.

Not Everyone Is Equally Receptive to Hypnosis

Finally, it's important to note that not everyone is equally receptive to hypnosis. We all fall somewhere on a spectrum from highly-hypnotizable to unhypnotizable, and so far, researchers have no idea why some people can be hypnotized and others can't. This will clearly affect whether hypnosis can play a part in your recovery.

While this seems like a clear strike against hypnosis as a treatment methodology, it's important to understand that the same applies to pretty much every treatment method. SSRI medications, for example, only work for about 40 to 60 percent of people with depression, but they remain an effective tool in the kit, and perhaps something similar is true of hypnosis.

Hypnosis isn't magic but it can cause in some patients major behavioral changes overnight and in some only minor changes over ap period of time , but it is an adjunct treatment method with ever-increasing scientific backing. If you're interested in trying hypnosis as part of therapy or addiction treatment, look for a therapist or addiction counselor with real training in hypnotherapy—ideally, one certified the oldest Society of Hypnotherapists (NGH) National Guild of Hypnotherapist. I am a proud member of this reputable society myself.

Materialism

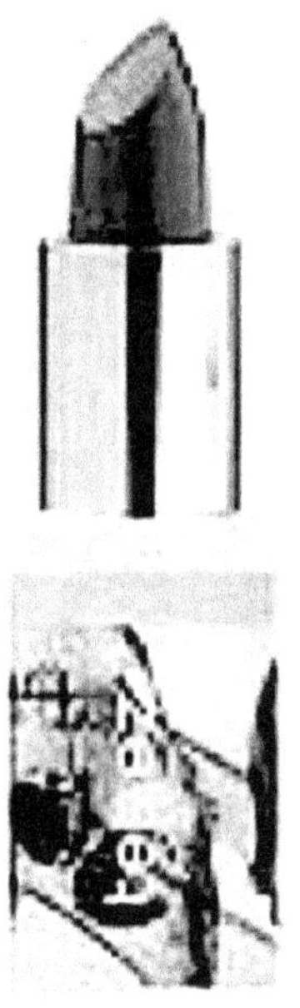

COPING SKILLS IN RECOVERY

Relapse is surprisingly prevalent, despite the fact that many people who suffer from addiction find a route to sobriety. In fact, 40–60 percent of patients who have entered addiction recovery have a relapse. While relapsing is inevitable, it can have life-threatening consequences in some cases. People who recover from addiction and begin misusing drugs and alcohol, for example, may be unaware that their tolerance has changed, and overdosing and even death can occur as a result. For this reason, adopting healthy coping skills in recovery is critical to maintaining sobriety. Learning these crucial strategies will not only help you avoid relapse but will also help you keep your commitment to a clean lifestyle.

What Are Coping Skills?

Coping skills are "any characteristic or behavioral pattern that enhances a person's adaptation." In other words, coping skills help you stay healthy when you are faced with a stressful circumstance. Sometimes, the coping mechanisms you develop are unhealthy. For example, you may use substances as your primary coping mechanism. In fact, many people actually turn to alcohol and drug abuse as a way to cope with underlying mental health issues.

If you have entered the recovery process, you need to find more appropriate coping skills. This will help you channel your energy into healthier outlets.

You should learn to recognize unhealthy and negative coping mechanisms. These include but are not limited to:

- Avoidance behaviors (not doing what needs to be done)
- Substance abuse, including smoking
- Spending too much
- Focusing on other's problems
- Sleeping all-day
- Over/undereating
- And more

COPING SKILLS YOU'LL LEARN IN RECOVERY

Understanding your triggers may be one of the first things you learn throughout addiction therapy. A good rehabilitation program will assist you in recognizing the patterns that lead to your addiction. You should be aware of your most risky triggers in order to avoid recurrence. These may include, but are not limited to, the following::

- Poor self-care (remember the acronym HALT: hungry, angry, lonely, tired)
- Isolation from others
- Negative thinking
- Stress
- Denial that you need help or avoid your problems
- Getting into your old patterns (i.e., hanging around friends who drink or use drugs)

We've created a list of some of the most frequent issues that people confront throughout recovery and some coping skills that might assist.

Negative Thinking

You may have heard this practice referred to as "stinking thinking" if you've ever attended a twelve-step program. This might involve the following:

- Complaining
- Being judgmental
- Blaming others
- Gossiping

While everyone is prone to the occasional negative thought, an excessive amount can become detrimental to relapse prevention.

Solution: Cognitive behavioral therapy helps you identify unhealthy thoughts (known as cognitive distortions) and respond to them in a productive way. During this type of talk therapy, you work with a mental health counselor, usually a psychotherapist or therapist, and come up with the required life skills to respond to cognitive distortions.

Stress

Stress is a well-known risk factor for addiction and can often increase your vulnerability to relapse. If you're in recovery, these stressors can include:

- Emotional abuse and physical abuse
- Loss of a job or home

- Death of a loved one
- Feeling isolated

Moreover, stressors do not have to be giant occurrences. Sometimes, all it takes is being late for work

Solution: There are a variety of stress management techniques you can incorporate into your life. For example, mindfulness meditation can help you see clearly through your problems and address them in a more beneficial manner. In addition, exercising and performing physical activities raises your endorphins, helping you to reduce stress and sleep better. Other activities to reduce stress include:

- Meditation
- Yoga
- Tai chi
- Massage
- Gardening
- Making a gratitude list
- Journaling and setting goals

Falling into Old Problems

Problem: When you make the choice to attain long-term recovery, you must be prepared to make changes in your life. If you don't remove yourself from the parts of your life that have exacerbated your condition, you may find your old behaviors catching up to you. Reframe your mindset so you see this as a chance to change your whole life for the better.

Solution: Keep a network of people in your life who are committed to helping you stay sober. This may include:

- Talking to counselors and therapists
- Attending support groups, including AA and NA
- Going back to rehab
- Having a reliable interpersonal network, including friends and family

Other Coping Strategies

Remember: what works for you may not work for someone else. Other coping mechanisms that may prove useful include:

- Practicing gratitude
- Keeping up with your faith or finding spirituality
- Eating healthy
- Attending anger management classes

UNHEALTHY COPING SKILLS IN RECOVERY

Bottling Up Your Feelings

Because they are terrified of showing vulnerability, some people prefer to bottle up their feelings. However, doing so may lead to you acting out in other ways, such as taking drugs or alcohol to cope with your emotions.

You may learn to better regulate your emotions by following the instructions below:

- Communicate your feelings consistently.

- Figure out why you keep your feelings inside.
- Accept and own your feelings.
- Write in a journal.
- Talk when you need to.
- Release your bottled feelings.

Hanging Out with Friends Who Use

If you're lonely, you could be tempted to return to your old behaviors. This can involve meeting with substance-abusing friends, family members, or coworkers. You must avoid these loved ones while you're still recovering. When you're invited to an event with some old pals, let them know about your situation. True friends will understand that you need time away, and your friendship will be strengthened due to this honesty. If your friends don't understand, you must create limits that tempt you to drink or take drugs. Instead of going to a bar or other establishment that provides alcohol, go to a coffee shop or juice bar.

HEALTHY COPING SKILLS TO PRACTICE IN RECOVERY

There are plenty of unhealthy coping skills you can practice while recovering from addiction, but these won't get you anywhere. Below are ten ways you can practice healthy coping skills in recovery.

Be Honest With Yourself

The most important thing you can do is be honest with yourself and others. If you're feeling anxious or depressed, be open about it, accept it, and own it. When you try to avoid your feelings; you can end up feeling worse. When you're honest with yourself, though, you can give yourself a break and realize that you're only human.

You're bound to come across things throughout the day that can make you upset. When, this happens, recognize your feelings and move on with the rest of the day.

Practice Gratitude and Keep a Daily Journal

When you're in recovery, it's important to remember what you're grateful for. Keep, a list each day of your thoughts, and reflect on what you're thankful for. This could include family, friends, a great job, and a roof over your head. Recalling moments throughout your day that bring you joy can make you generally happier and will make your recovery easier.

Practice Meditation

Mindfulness meditation helps us become more self-aware. It will help you make better choices each day and react appropriately to substance cravings. Your anxiety and stress will decrease, and this will lower your potential for relapse. When you do feel stressed or anxious, meditating can also help you take back control of your feelings and realign yourself.

Attend Therapy Sessions

Many recovering addicts can attest that therapy has saved their lives. Individual, group, and family therapy while in treatment help you overcome the worst of your addiction. However, therapy after treatment is also important. Discussing your struggles in recovery with a mental health professional will take some of your burdens away. This third-party observer can help you make sense of your feelings.

Surround Yourself with a Support System

We mentioned earlier that having friends and family who support your recovery is essential. Joining twelve-step support groups like Alcoholics Anonymous or Narcotics Anonymous can also help since they expose you to fellow recovering addicts. These people know what you're going through and can offer support and insight.

Support groups will provide you with a sponsor who has been in recovery for years and can offer you a helping hand. This is especially helpful when cravings come along.

Learn To Relax

We encounter many high-stress situations, whether we're at work, school, or home. One of the best ways to decompress is to learn how to relax in any situation. Take a long bath or listen to soothing music after a long day. Yoga can also help you relax your mind while strengthening your body.

Meditation is an excellent relaxation technique as well. Take a walk, watch your favorite TV show, or sit on the beach and listen to the sounds of the ocean. When you practice guided imagery, you can imagine yourself in a relaxing place, too.

Eat Right and Exercise Regularly

When you take care of your body, it will thank you. What you consume has an incredible effect on your mental health, which is why you should eat healthy, nutrient-rich foods. Part of addiction comes from malnourishment and not giving your body what it really needs. Make sure to stay hydrated at all times.

Exercising can also release endorphins in your brain, and this makes you feel great. It also adds structure to your day, and having a routine is key to staying sober. Taking care of your body by exercising and eating right will yield untold benefits.

Do Activities You Enjoy

Do you like kayaking? Volunteering? Making short films? Then do it! Throwing yourself in an activity that brings you joy and helps others can give you a sense of accomplishment. When you're fully engaged in something, you're not thinking about drugs and alcohol. Keeping yourself busy in recovery can help you see what's most important in life.

RELAPSE TRIGGERS

Relapse triggers are people, places, things, and feelings that remind you of your previous substance abuse. These can bring about urges and cravings that can result in relapse. People who have used drugs for a long time associate substance use with feeling good. Even after you get sober, these associations will still be there, and when you encounter triggers, you're bound to crave drugs and alcohol.

Whether you've abstained from substances for two months or two years, you must be aware of triggers that set off your cravings.

External Triggers

External triggers are physical things that remind you of past drug use. Some examples of external triggers include:

1. People: Those closest to you (friends, family, coworkers, former drug dealers) can be triggers that cause you to relapse. You shouldn't be around loved ones who have substance use disorder.

2. Places: Walking or driving by a location where you used to drink or use drugs can set off cravings. These can include bars, restaurants, neighborhoods, bathrooms, and hotels. Try to avoid these places by using an alternative route to get to your destination.

3. Objects: Even material things can spark cravings. Drug paraphernalia, spoons (for heroin users), and empty pill bottles are all things that can influence a recovering addict's behavior.

4. Activities/Situations: Stressful situations can push those in recovery over the edge. These don't just include losing a job or a loved one. Joyous occasions like weddings, birthdays, and other parties where alcohol is flowing can also induce cravings. Other situational triggers include:

- Calls from creditors
- Payday
- Before, during, and after sex
- Being home alone
- Eating lunch or dinner
- Talking on the phone

Internal Triggers

Internal triggers are emotions, feelings, and thoughts that you associate with drug use. These are harder to manage than external triggers because you can't always avoid them. Internal triggers can lead to negative behavior that eventually leads to relapse.

Examples of internal triggers include:

- Negative Feelings: If you ever feel irritated, angry, jealous, or anxious, you may think about turning to drugs and alcohol for comfort.

- Normal feelings: You might not think it, but even normal feelings can be triggers. Relaxation, boredom, embarrassment, and neglect can make you think about using.

- Positive feelings: Feeling excited, happy, confident, and strong can also lead to relapse. Celebrating something could make you want to reach for a bottle and join in on the fun.

To recognize which feelings could potentially set off a relapse, ask yourself the following questions: How do I feel before using substances?

- How do I want to feel before using drugs and alcohol?
- How did I feel when I used or wanted to use drugs and alcohol in the last week?

Creating A Relapse Prevention Plan

A good relapse prevention plan might include some elements of the following:

- Daily exercise
- Daily meditation
- Praying or other forms of spirituality
- Daily journaling
- Practicing a hobby like crocheting or learning a new instrument
- Finishing everything on your to-do list every day
- Reach out to a sponsor if you encounter a trigger or just need to talk

What If I Relapse?

If you relapse, don't consider it a failure. Although you've suffered a setback, it doesn't mean that there isn't hope left for you. Everyone encounters obstacles on their road to success. Relapse is more common than you think; most people in recovery return to drug and alcohol use within one year of completing treatment.

You might have to enter treatment again if your situation is dire. However, by attending support groups like Alcoholics Anonymous or Narcotics Anonymous and participating in aftercare programs, you should get back on the right track soon enough.

Materialisim

My-mindguide.com

BREAK FREE FROM MATERIALISM

Money can't buy you, love. It can't buy you happiness either. Today's materialistic world often urges us to buy the coolest gadgets; the trendiest clothes; and bigger, better things, but research shows that possessions and purchases don't buy our happiness.

By and large, money buys happiness only for those who lack the basic needs. Once you pass an income of $50,000, more money doesn't buy much more happiness.

So while we're being pushed toward materialism, it's for monetary gain by corporations, not for our own happiness. Unfortunately, it's brutal to escape the trap of materialism and find happiness in other ways than buying stuff online or finding joy in the mall.

How many times have you heard the complaint that we live in a materialistic world? Are you guilty of being materialistic? If yes, wouldn't you want to get out of that vicious cycle accumulating material possessions, only to be left wanting even more after getting what you originally wanted?

Unfortunately, it is indeed a very materialistic world that we live in today. Social experts say that despite the increasing wealth of today's society, people aren't necessarily happier. Why? Because the old adage that materialism breeds discontent holds true, today more than ever.

In the next sections, we will have a quick glare on how to actually break free from it.

But it's possible. Here's a guide to finding a materialism-free life and discovering true happiness.

ENHANCE YOUR WELL-BEING BY FOCUSING ON DEEPER GOALS

All around us, there are messages telling us to buy stuff. On the Internet (blogs included), we see continuous advertising trying to get us to purchase a product or service. It's the main reason for television and movies: constant product placement! Hence, we aren't always sure what is advertising and what was put in there by the director.

Flip on the radio or open up a newspaper or magazine, and you're bombarded with more advertising. Go to a shopping center/mall, and the urge to buy comes from every direction.

This message to continually buy, buy, buy . . . and the notion that it will somehow make us happpier . . . is drilled into our heads from the days of Happy Meals and cartoons until the day we die. It's inescapable.

Well, almost. You could go and live in a cabin in the woods (and that actually sounds nice), or you could still live in our modern society, but find ways to escape materialism. Here are some suggestions:

Limit Television

Do you really enjoy watching TV for hours? Think about which shows you really, really love, and only watch during that time. When the commercials come on, go do something else. Or use Tivo to watch TV. You can even give up cable TV entirely, if you're brave—I have, and it's one of the best things I've ever done.

Eschew the News

Journalists will never tell you this, but when they're sincere (behind closed doors), they'll confess that the most important part of any news company, from TV or radio news to Internet or print news, is the advertising division. It's the division that pays the company's bills. The news is important, too . . . in driving traffic to the advertising. So, when you're watching or reading news, you're really being sucked into advertising. Try this instead: boycott the news for a week. I've done it for about two years, and it hasn't hurt me a bit. In fact, it's helped me a lot.

Limit Internet Reading

I'm not saying you should cancel your cable Internet subscription or anything. I love reading blogs. But find just those that you truly love reading that give you the most value, and limit your reading to those. And just do it once a day, for thirty minutes or so. If you can do that, you've gone a long way towards tearing yourself away from advertising.

Give up magazines for books. Magazines are also designed with advertising in mind. And they rarely give you much value. Try reading an ad-free book instead. It's a much better use of your time.

Don't Go to the Mall

The only purpose of these places is for you to spend money. If you just want a place to spend your Saturday afternoon, find a location where you don't need to spend money to have fun—a park or a beach, for example. If you need to buy something, go to a single store (not the mall), go in, and get what you need. Don't browse and walk around looking at stuff. You'll get sucked in.

Monitor Your Urges

When you're online, watching TV, or at a store, keep track of the number of times you want to buy something. Keep a little notebook or index card, and just put tally marks. Once you become more aware of your urges to buy things, you can start to control them. If you could control them, limiting your consumption of media (see above tips) isn't necessary—although I would argue that it still gives you a better quality of life.

Use a Thirty-Day List

I've said it before, but I'll say it again—because this one works wonders! If you really want to buy something, put it on a list and write down the date you added the item to the list. Now tell yourself you can't buy that item for thirty days. It might be difficult, but you can do it. When the thirty days have passed, if you still want it, *then* buy it. But you can't buy anything (besides essentials like groceries) without putting it on the list for thirty days first. Many times, our urges to buy something will pass during this waiting period.

Declutter

I find it pretty amazing to see all the crap I buy over a period of years, when I go through my closets and other possessions and start getting rid of stuff I don't use or want anymore. It's a gratifying process, and at the same time, it makes me realize how useless all of our consumer shopping is. I don't need *any* of the stuff! When you do this, you may be less likely to buy more stuff. Especially if you enjoy the decluttered look of your house as much as I do.

Find Other Forms of Entertainment

There are other things to do besides watching TV or movies or reading magazines, newspapers, or the things on the Internet. Try playing sports or exercising. Try playing board games or creating art or writing a book. Try doing fun things with your kids or visiting relatives and other loved ones. Try volunteering with a charity. I'm sure you could come up with a hundred free or cheap things to do.

Buy Used

When you get the urge to buy something and you're convinced that it's needed, try finding it used instead of new. Look in thrift shops or garage sales or flea markets or similar places.

A True Path to Happiness

So, if you're able to escape materialism, how can you find true happiness? There are many ways, and each of us is different, but here are some things I suggest trying:

Gratitude List: Make a list of things about which you're grateful in your life. Give thanks for them daily.

Think Positive: Try eliminating negative thinking from your life, adopting a more positive outlook.

Small Pleasures: Make a list of small things that give you great pleasure. Sprinkle them throughout your day. Notice other small pleasures as you go through your day.

Kindness: Practice random acts of kindness and compassion. Do it anonymously. Help those in need. Volunteer. Make someone smile.

Love: Make an intimate connection with your loved one. Develop your friendships. Spend time with others, converse, understand them, and make them happy.

Exercise: It sounds trite, but it can bring great happiness to your life.

Meaning: It's often useful to find meaning, either through a church or spiritual way, or through those we love in life or through the things we're passionate about. Give yourself a purpose.

Flow: Eliminate distractions, and really pour yourself into whatever you're doing. If it's writing an article, like this one, really put yourself into it, until you forget the outside world.

Know Yourself: Become attuned to what brings you happiness. Study yourself. Learn about what you love, and about your ability to love—increase your capacity for compassion.

Reducing Materialism

You reducing your penchant for materialism doesn't mean forsaking all of your possessions. Ridding yourself of everything you own would only prove you are still too preoccupied with possessions themselves. Someone who has developed a healthy inner world would see possessions as neutral. This shift is more about attitude than specific actions. Here are some ideas to get you started:

You Aren't the Things You Own

The problem is that you view things as possessions in the first place. Ownership is just a societal construct to keep order; it doesn't have any deeper meaning. Separate your identity from the things you own.

Relationships Are About Doing, Not Having

You can't "have" a girlfriend, boyfriend, or spouse. Although those terms are fairly commonplace, they demonstrate that many people still view relationships as possessions. The more you see relationships as possessions, the less intrinsic value you can get from experiencing them.

Create a System of Goals and Challenges

Materialism occupies a void. Replace that uncomfortable filler with goals and challenges. Although many of my challenges are directed towards material gain, that isn't the real point. Just as winning *Risk* isn't about world-domination; it's about a fun challenge.

Serve

Invest your energies into helping other people. I don't view acts as being on a continuum from selfishness to selflessness, as acts that directly benefit me can benefit others as well. But even in that case, shifting your focus onto the needs of others, can replace materialism.

Trash It

I'm the opposite of a packrat. When I need to do a major cleaning, I usually toss just about everything I haven't used recently. Getting rid of old possessions can be a liberating experience, stripping away what isn't important.

See Wealth as a Challenge, Not a Result

I view earning more money as an interesting and complex game. I expect my minimum comfort threshold would only to be around $15,000 to $20,000 per year—beyond that, earning more is simply a bigger challenge.

Experience Over Objects

The only reason to buy an object is because you believe it will (directly or indirectly) improve the quality of your experience. Going straight to the source helps you avoid the "middlemen" represented by material goods.

Build Intangible Assets

Habits, time-management, discipline, emotional control, understanding, and learning are just a few of the non-physical assets you can hold. Building intangible assets replaces your need for physical ones.

Use Money to Free, Not Shackle Yourself

When you have a larger income, don't simply adapt by increasing your lifestyle. Instead, work to create a buffer between your income and lifestyle so you live below your means. This will give you more freedom to pursue goals and ideas that may not immediately contribute to your productivity.

Go Basic

Simplify all your material possessions so they don't consume your mental resources. Simple, even if less glamorous, requires less maintenance, offers fewer distractions and uses less thinking. A simple lifestyle affords you the ability to focus your energies on your inner world.

Avoid the Status Game

Seek friends from all social layers. Don't buy into the game that decides a person's worth based on their income or profession. I know people I would consider smarter and more enlightened who live on a fraction of the income that others do. Keeping pockets of connections within all levels separates you from the competitive aspects materialism brings.

Judge Yourself by Your Ethics and Your Understanding

I'd be far happier with myself if I were poor with a strong sense of morals than rich but devoid of scruples. Don't base your self-worth on how much you've achieved or the admiration of your peers.

Let Go

Buddhism teaches that attachment to things creates suffering. Again, this is all a matter of one's mindset. I'm not a Buddhist, but as I understand it, this doesn't mean the only path to true happiness is to abandon everything. It simply means that you stop trying to hold on to all the things you "own," including other people.

You can't take anything with you. What is it going to matter to you on your deathbed? Looking back at your entire life, what will stand out as most important? Use that to prioritize.

My-mindguide.com

REGRESSION THERAPY FOR MATERIALISM ADDICTION

Regression therapy is an approach to treatment that focuses on resolving significant past events that interfere with a person's present mental and emotional wellness.

Therapists who practice this approach believe people seeking treatment for phobias, depression, intimacy issues, and a range of other concerns can see improvement in their state of mind by revisiting and reliving the early experiences that influenced the development of these issues. However, the approach is somewhat controversial due to limited research supporting the method and the potential for false memories.

History and Development

Regression therapy primarily developed out of the theories and techniques of hypnotherapy and psychoanalysis, with their emphasis on rediscovering details of past events in order to solve current conflicts and emotions. Hypnotherapy and psychoanalysis both rose in popularity in the 1950s as the field of psychology began to embrace the belief that the past was the cause of turmoil in people's lives.

Sigmund Freud, who developed the concept of bringing the unconscious to the conscious, was a prominent figure during the growth of psychoanalysis, and many of his ideas informed the development of regression therapy. Morris Netherton, who published *Past Lives Therapy*, the first book in the field of regression therapy, in 1978, has taught his theories in regression therapy across the world. Brian Weiss, who is credited with the continued development of regression therapy techniques since the 1980s, is another prominent figure in the field.

Theory and Principles

As the works of psychoanalysis and hypnotherapy came together to inform regression therapy, consciousness became a central component to the work of regression therapists, and the psychoanalytical view of consciousness having three levels was adopted by regression therapy.

The three levels of consciousness recognized in regression therapy are as follows:

1. The conscious mind, which represents the thoughts a person is aware of having

2. The subconscious mind, which represents emotions, habits, and instincts a person is unaware of having

3. The super conscious mind, also known as the spirit, soul, or higher element of a person, which may provide a model for how that person wants to think or act in the world

Regression therapy holds that as a person moves through life, they collect memories that are then stored in the mind. Some of these memories are accessible to the conscious mind.

Still, other memories may remain in the subconscious, and a person is generally unable to bring details of those memories to the conscious awareness without aid. Even though the subconscious memories aren't able to be accessed, regression therapists believe they can still have a significant impact on a person's development and ability to function in daily life.

Types of Regression Therapy

These are some of the different approaches to regression therapy:

- Hypnotic Regression Therapy: While all types of regression therapy involve hypnosis, this most general type does not necessarily include mentions of past lives or year-by-year age regression. It intends to help patients access their subconscious minds through hypnosis.

- Age Regression Therapy: In this type of regression therapy, therapists induce amnesia in the patient and then ask them to return to past years. According to the American Psychological Association, this remains controversial in the psychiatric community due to the potential for false memories.

- Past-Life Regression Therapy: This hinges on the belief that we carry over many of our traumas from our past lives. This is very controversial and, according to the American Psychological Association, not recognized by many hypnotherapists.

HOW DOES REGRESSION THERAPY WORK?

Regression therapy focuses on areas of conflict and other potentially unpleasant aspects of a person's life to identify and determine the sources of negative emotions to be addressed more effectively.

Hypnotic regression therapy often occurs in five phases:
- Preparation
- Conducting regression techniques
- Expression and release of previously repressed emotions
- Relearning/Reprogramming of the subconscious
- Session conclusion

The regression therapist helps the person enter into a relaxed state via deep breathing. The role of the therapist then becomes to facilitate the process of regression as the person closes their eyes and speaks out loud about a past significant experience, urging them to be as detailed as possible about their surroundings and any sensory feelings that come up in the process. The therapist may also prompt the individual, if necessary, to speak about any emotions that arise as the event is re-experienced. It's believed that through this process, a person can access their subconscious mind and isolate the emotions associated with the past event.

Once these emotions are isolated and brought to the conscious mind, the therapist and person can begin to identify possible ways they may be having a harmful impact. In the relearning/reprogramming phase, the therapist and person in treatment work together to develop alternative ways of describing the past event that better promote a sense of resilience and foster adaptive strengths in the person.

Regression therapy can be practiced through a therapist-directed or person-centered approach. Therapist-directed trance work requires less training in hypnosis, as therapists often use a script, to fit the concern of the person seeking help. These scripts may be helpful in some instances, but they also may leave certain issues unaddressed. Many practitioners find this to be a less effective method than person-centered hypnotic regression therapy, in which the therapist uses hypnosis to allow the person in treatment the opportunity to obtain answers for themselves. Current practitioners of regression therapy typically adapt techniques, Gestalt therapy practices and inner child work among them, to provide the best care for the specific issues of the person they are treating.

Some regression therapists practice past-life regression, which considers the possibility of past-life memories. That said, regression therapists largely use regression therapy to look at significant memories from the earlier stages of a person's life.

Who Offers Regression Therapy?

Regression therapy is a specialized type of therapy that involves specific training and experience. A primary tenet of the approach is the concept of core levels of consciousness, many regression therapists have a background in psychoanalysis. It's recommended that therapists who wish to offer regression therapy seek thorough training in the practice of hypnotherapy, as when hypnosis, like any method of treatment, is used without adequate training, it carries the potential for harm.

The International Board for Regression Therapy is a governing body that provides accreditation to therapy programs, certification in regression therapy, and continuing education for practitioners. The Earth Association for Regression Therapy is another worldwide organization that offers training in this approach, and many of their recognized trainers offer advanced workshops in different parts of the world.

HOW CAN REGRESSION THERAPY HELP?

Regression therapy has been used successfully with individuals of varying ages and backgrounds. One area in which some consider regression therapy to be particularly useful is in the treatment of significant traumas. Proponents of regression therapy believe a traumatic event can often have a continued impact on a person's ability to express emotion and interact with other people, though the personal may not readily recall the details of the trauma. Regression therapy can, then, be of benefit, because it can help a person return to trauma in order to understand the impact the trauma may be having on their behaviors and choices.

Proponents of the approach believe regression can be highly effective when individuals experience one or more of the of the following symptoms:

- Fears or phobias that have no recognized cause
- Intimacy issues

- General relationship issues
- Feelings of guilt and shame that seem to have no explanation.

Regression therapy is a shorter approach to treatment: some people may see results after only one or two sessions.

CONCERNS AND LIMITATIONS

Scientific research supporting the efficacy of regression therapy is limited, and this approach is somewhat controversial. Research does indicate that hypnosis is a significant factor in the development of false memories, and there have been a number of cases studied in which individuals "uncovered," through regression therapy, memories of abuse or other trauma that were later found to be false.

It is generally advised that therapists practice regression therapy in such a way that they guide the person through the re-experiencing process with open-ended questions, such as "What do you see, hear, or feel?" rather than lead the person by asking questions that may be suggestive or generate "memories" of an event that didn't take place.

Past-life regression therapy, an approach to treatment where the person seeking help is encouraged to consider the possibility of a "past life," has been shown to have some psychological benefit in cases where the person in treatment believes in the possibility of past lives. However, this method is also considered controversial.

HEALING FROM THE PAST AND LIVING IN THE PRESENT

Our past shapes our present and helps us identify who we are and where we're headed. So, it's natural to use our past experiences as a point of reference for our current situation. The choices we make for ourselves today are often influenced by our past. If we are using healthy judgment to guide our choices, then past regrets, mistakes, and pain are used as markers for what we don't want in our lives. However for some, the past is not seen as a place of reflection but as a destination. For those who struggle with letting go of past pain or regret, they can feel trapped by their situation and unable to move forward in their lives. Feeling unable to let go of the past can lead to clinical depression, post-traumatic stress disorder (PTSD), or even suicide

What is Trauma?

Traumatic events that take place both in our youth and adulthood can cause permanent changes in our psychological and physical responses to stress. The term 'trauma' describes any unforeseen circumstance where a person's emotional or physical well-being is disturbed by the stress of the situation. Any situation can result in trauma, though common examples include:

- Witnessing death
- Emotional neglect or abuse
- Physical injury
- Natural disasters

Once a traumatic event has occurred, it is normal and healthy for a person to experience grief or sadness for a certain period of time. However, some people develop distressing symptoms that persist for longer than they should. These symptoms end up overwhelming a person's ability to live a normal and healthy life. Additionally, the symptoms don't seem to wane as time goes on.

Pain has a way of making us feel stuck. In times of emotional pain, we may find ourselves thinking back to when we felt happier, which can help motivate us in the present. For example, if in the past we were proud of a personal accomplishment, thinking of our past success can help motivate us in achieving new successes now. Referencing our past positive experiences can be a healthy option for setting goals or in building optimal habits as we focus on our future. While a little reflection can be healthy and foster creativity, too much reflection or ruminating on past negative experiences can drift into obsession and lead to feeling stuck.

Our past experiences can affect our current mindset and our choices in how we interpret our lives. If pain or trauma has been experienced in our past, it can impact how we view our current circumstances or even prevent us from living in the present. Existing research suggests how negative experiences are often associated with increased incidences of trait anxiety, depression, impulsivity, low self-esteem, and poor choices. For example, if we have suffered betrayal from a loved one in a romantic or familial relationship, we may re-live the traumatic experience as it replays in our mind. Certain smells, foods, places or songs may "trigger" re-experiencing the pain, which often results in trying to push away the intrusive thoughts and feelings. This can lead to other symptoms including social isolation, distrust in others, self-sabotaging behavior and an inability to move ahead in our lives (i.e., living in the past).

Warning Signs of Living in the Past:
- Conversations revert to certain times, certain people, or specific situations
- You're attracted to the same type of people that cause you pain
- Disagreements often surround past arguments
- Easily bored or frustrated
- You're comparing your current situation to previous ones
- Prior trauma or painful events replay in your mind
- Self-sabotaging behavior
- Relationships are used to fill a void or prevent being alone with your thoughts
- "Waiting for the other shoe to drop"—expecting something terrible to happen and feeling anxious or acting impulsively.
- Feelings of regret over impulsive choices
- All-or-nothing thinking about new people and/or new experiences
- Avoidance of new people or new experiences

Self-Sabotaging Behavior
Many times, the hallmark of living in the past is a pattern of self-sabotaging behavior that reinforces reliving past

traumatic events. What makes behavior self-sabotaging is how it negatively affects the person in its aftermath. Self-sabotaging behavior usually starts out as a way to reduce or avoid unpleasant feelings, such as those that we endure when re-experiencing something painful. In an attempt to push away intrusive thoughts or vulnerable emotions, things like self-medicating, escape/avoidant behaviors, or other unhealthy patterns can form. For example, a history of being abandoned result in one abandoning partners or friends—or lashing out at them when feeling emotionally vulnerable. This pattern can lead to a history of unhealthy relationships and a toxic cycle that perpetuates the avoidance pain by way of self-sabotaging behavior.

What Are the Different Types of Trauma?

PTSD

When the anxiety and stress from a traumatic event become chronic, significantly disrupting the way a person lives, the individual may be diagnosed with PTSD. PTSD occurs when the body's normal psychological defences against stress become overwhelming. There is a noticeable dysfunction with the normal defense systems after the trauma, which causes certain symptoms.

Acute Stress Disorder

Acute Stress Disorder shares many similarities with PTSD. However, it is diagnosed when symptoms have been present between three and thirty days. Symptoms of acute stress disorder include disturbing memories, feeling detached, issues with concentration, avoidance, and a negative mood. People with acute stress disorder may also feel a lot of guilt about not stopping the trauma or for not being able to move on from it quickly.

Developmental Trauma

Developmental trauma describes a wide range of adverse events that take place during childhood, such as abuse (sexual, physical, or emotional), rejection, betrayal, being abandoned, or witnessing death or violence. Individuals who experience developmental trauma have an increased risk of developing mental health conditions such as PTSD.

Complex PTSD

Complex PTSD is a term that often describes the results of numerous experiences of developmental trauma. Survivors of these experiences may have deeply-rooted negative beliefs about themselves and even the world. They are used to being in a mode of survival. They often fluctuate between feeling numb and experiencing intense emotional states that leave them overwhelmed by their feelings. It is also common for those with Complex PTSD to believe that no one understands them.

HOW TO HEAL FROM THE PAST

Healing from past pain or traumatic experiences doesn't happen overnight. It's a process that requires patience, dedication and a commitment to change. Humans are wired to seek pleasure and to minimize pain, which often triggers self-sabotaging behavior in an attempt to avoid negative feelings. When we experience a painful event such as betrayal or other traumatic experiences, it can rewire us for self-preservation.

We may live in "fight or flight" mode, constantly anticipating more pain in our lives which can be unconsciously welcomed through our actions.

Tips for Learning to Live in the Present

Establish Boundaries

This can mean something different for everyone, but the main point is to give yourself time to heal and to move ahead at your own pace. For many, establishing boundaries may include being more selective about who they welcome into their lives and whom they dismiss. With boundaries, consistency is key in helping let go of the past and living in the present.

Acceptance

The past is a done-deal. We can't change it. And being stuck in the past is only hurting our potential in the present. By accepting that the past is over, it allows us to grieve and to release the pain that we may have been carrying with us—be honest with yourself in your acceptance and take the time you need to grieve.

Practice Mindfulness

The practice of mindfulness is about teaching ourselves how to stay in the present and to calm our mind when experiencing emotional triggers. Research supports the use of mindfulness as part of a comprehensive program in healing from trauma, depression, or PTSD.

Have a Reset Button

We are human, and that means we are perfectly imperfect, and as such, all new skills take time to develop and master. Be kind to yourself if you slip up, find yourself reliving the past, or reverting back to old behavior patterns. Use the reset button to help you gauge where you are in your personal development.

Disconnect

Balance is key when working on self-improvement. Being okay with disconnecting from social media while you work on healing is about self-care. When we're alone, we're able to get to know ourselves and give ourselves the attention and love we need to stop living in the past.

How Do You Know If Someone Is Suffering from Trauma?

Even though the symptoms and causes of trauma vary, there are some typical signs of trauma that others can look out for. People who have experienced traumatic events typically appear disoriented and shaken. They may also have a hard time responding to a conversation as they would normally and often seem withdrawn or distant, even when they are speaking.

Another telling sign of a victim of trauma is anxiety. Anxiety caused by trauma can cause issues such as irritability, edginess, mood swings, poor concentration, and night terrors. Even though these symptoms are quite common; they're not all-inclusive. People respond to trauma in various ways.

Sometimes even friends and family members can't tell that a loved one is suffering from trauma. That's why it's important to talk to someone following a traumatic event, even if they don't display any signs of disturbance. In fact, it can take days, months and even years for trauma to manifest following the actual event.

Emotional Trauma Symptoms

Trauma usually manifests through emotion, such as anger, denial, emotional outbursts, and sadness. Trauma victims may redirect their feelings toward friends, family members, and other sources.

Physical Trauma Symptoms

A physical manifestation of trauma is also common. Common physical signs of trauma may include fatigue, lethargy, paleness, poor concentration and an increased heartbeat. The victim may experience panic attacks or anxiety. They may also have a hard time coping in certain situations. The physical symptoms of trauma can be as real as symptoms of an illness or physical injury.

What Are the Short- and Long-Term Effects of Trauma?

Effects of trauma either take place over a short period, several weeks, or even years. It is crucial to address any effects of trauma in order to prevent permanence. A person's chance of successful and complete recovery is influenced by the time it takes for the trauma to be addressed. While short-term and long-term effects may have their similarities, long-term effects are often more severe.

Short-term mood changes are to be expected after trauma, but it may result in a long-term effect if the changes last for more than a few weeks.

How is Trauma Diagnosed?

For a person to be diagnosed with trauma, they don't have to have all the symptoms previously mentioned. In fact, most people don't even experience the entire array of symptoms. To diagnose trauma, doctors and mental health professionals usually perform a physical examination to determine whether medical problems may be causing symptoms. Then, they conduct a psychological evaluation. This involves discussing one's signs and symptoms as well as the event(s) that led up to them.

Mental health professionals examine the way that various issues affect a person's daily life and influence behaviors or habits in a negative or lasting way. A therapist watches for situations or words that may trigger the person's symptoms, along with ongoing emotions or moods related to the stress response.

How Are Trauma and Co-Occurring Mental Health Conditions Linked?

It is common for trauma and PTSD to be accompanied by other mental health issues. Some increase the likelihood of PTSD occurring after a traumatic event while others may be a result of PTSD symptoms. In some cases, they may be completely unrelated. Typical mental health conditions that are linked to trauma include substance abuse, anxiety, depression, and grief.

It can be more difficult for a person to get help if trauma is complicated by other mental health issues, which is why it is crucial to find a trauma treatment center or professional who specializes in dual diagnosis or co-occurring disorders.

WHAT IS TRAUMA TREATMENT

The path to recovery from trauma and PTSD is different for each person. Inpatient trauma treatment and counselling can help individuals understand their feelings and experiences, learn healthy coping skills, connect with support and other resources, and ultimately grow from their traumatic experience.

Some of the most successful methods used at a trauma treatment centre include cognitive-behavioral therapy (CBT) and eye movement desensitization and reprocessing (EMDR). Individuals might also join group therapy sessions, which can help them heal by addressing questions that arise following trauma.

Most people who receive trauma treatment make a successful recovery. In cases where inpatient trauma treatment is not effective, it is often because a person-centered approach is not used. Likewise, co-occurring mental health issues may not have been effectively addressed.

TRAUMA THERAPY TECHNIQUES?

There is no one-size-fits-all technique to trauma therapy, but it is possible to identify the proper technique or combination of methods for an individual. Even though a trauma treatment center may utilize a variety of approaches, they all have the same objective of integrating the traumatic incident into the person's life rather than removing it. At a residential trauma treatment center, the following strategies are some of the most common and effective forms of therapy.

Trauma-Focused Cognitive Behavioural Therapy (TF-CBT)

TF-CBT is an evidence-based treatment program that helps individuals deal with the aftermath of a traumatic experience. While CBT provides effective methods for promoting healing and treating trauma-related issues, TF-CBT uses a trauma-sensitive approach and other expanded methods. The TF-CBT approach encourages clients to discuss their feelings and aims to help people who have experienced trauma learn how to manage difficult or painful emotions in a healthier way.

Eye Movement Desensitisation and Reprocessing (EMDR)

EMDR sessions follow a preset sequence of eight phases or steps. Treatment requires the individual in trauma therapy or inpatient trauma treatment to mentally focus on the traumatic experience or negative thought while tracking the therapist's movement of a finger or a moving light before their eyes. In some cases, auditory tones are also used. It helps people heal from symptoms related to traumatic memories and improves distress by assisting them to view the event in a less disturbing way. By comprising bi-lateral eye movements, the technique helps move painful memories from the forefront of the mind into the long-term memory.

Other useful trauma therapy techniques that are often used in a residential trauma treatment centre include:

Trauma Resiliency Model (TRM) Skill-Building

TRM is a somatic, or body-based, therapy that resets the disturbed nervous system of individuals suffering from trauma. Clients learn how to watch and track their nervous system responses when they feel depressed, stressed or anxious so they are able to balance themselves when this responses occur.

Mindfulness-Based Cognitive Therapy (MBCT)
MBCT helps people mindfully recognise and become in tune with their negative feelings, thoughts and bodily sensations.

Trauma-Releasing Exercises (TRE) Yoga
TRE yoga helps release stress or tension that is associated with trauma through exercises that release "triggered" muscles as a result of a fight-or-flight response. In fact, these muscles often remain contracted until the initial trauma has been resolved.

Group Therapy
There are many different groups for people dealing with trauma. Both therapists and peers can lead group sessions. Some focus on giving support while others serve an educational purpose. Group therapy is most effective when it's issued in tandem with individual therapy.

REAL-LIFE STORY

Anxiety and Other Consequences of Childhood Abuse
Pat, a fifty-two-year-old man, describes himself as a person who is highly anxious. In an attempt to overcome his anxiety, he seeks therapy. After discussing Pat's history, the therapist discovers that Pat was severely physically abused when he was young. Pat finds it difficult to discuss the topic, so the therapist doesn't force or push him to revisit the events but finds a way to gently bring it up in the following sessions.

When this happens, Pat starts to become angry and upset. Upon observing his reaction, Pat agrees that his response shows that the abuse still has an effect on him, which he hasn't thoroughly addressed. Pat's therapist recommends EMDR therapy and describes how it works. With the therapist's suggestion, Pat starts EMDR sessions, which help him acknowledge the abuse in a somewhat passive way. Once Pat openly confronts his abusive past, he begins to heal from it. As a result, his anxiety slowly starts to diminish until it is significantly less.

Readjusting to Civilian Life

Richard is a twenty-seven-year-old man who recently served in Iran, where he was involved in heavy combat. He ensures his therapist that he was fine until a week before their session when a robbery took place in a local store he was visiting. All of a sudden, he was overcome by graphic recollections of his time in Iran. Since then, he has had nightmares about being in combat.

Richard feels anxious and overwhelmed about these flashbacks. He also feels guilty about the fact that he survived while his two friends did not. On top of that, he has guilt about not preventing the robbery, having adopted acts of bravery as his responsibility. During his therapy sessions, Richard feels some relief after discussing his feelings. Another thing that helps is concentrating on ways to stay safe.

The therapist addresses Richard's guilt by getting him to explore his views on what being a veteran means as well as the high expectations he has of himself. Through therapy, Richard learns some grounding and relaxation exercises. He also asks for a psychiatric referral for anti-anxiety medications to help with sleep. Richard chooses to join veteran group therapy with others who are dealing with similar issues.

A year after his initial therapy sessions, Richard no longer needs to take medication and is starting to feel more hopeful, even though he still experiences intense grief about the war from time to time.

DO PEOPLE RECOVER FROM TRAUMA?

If stress, anxiety and other issues following a traumatic event are affecting your life, it is important to see a mental health professional or doctor as soon as possible. The following actions are also beneficial to the treatment of trauma:

Learn about Trauma and PTSD
Knowing more about your condition helps you understand why you're feeling the way you are, allowing you to create effective coping strategies.

Avoid Self-Medication
Using drugs or alcohol to numb what you're feeling is far from healthy, even though it may seem tempting. Additionally, it can interfere with treatments you are receiving from a trauma treatment center and get in the way of real healing.

Spend Time with Others
Spending time with people who care about and support you helps you heal, even if you don't discuss what happened. Simply sharing time with people who love you offers great comfort.

Find a Support Group

Ask a therapist or mental health professional to help you find a support group, or search online for one in your area.

Seek Help at a Trauma Treatment Centre

Even though you might not feel the benefits of therapy right away, treatment at a residential trauma treatment center can be effective. Remember that many people make a successful recovery and that these things take time. Follow your trauma treatment plan and openly communicate with your therapists or mental health professionals.

Practice Self-Care

Self-care reduces stress. Equally important, it feels good. Practice self-care throughout your healing journey by regularly taking action to do things that feel good and loving yourself.

Self-care acts can be simple and free and might be as mundane as taking a bath. What matters is setting time aside to care for yourself and doing things that make you feel loved.

Take Breaks

When moving through healing, you might find that you're more tired than usual. Or, you might feel that you have physical energy but your mind doesn't work as well. Healing from trauma takes a lot of energy.

The best way to deal with reduced energy during this time, whether physical or mental, is to be gentle with yourself. Taking breaks, even from doing fun things, to pause and give yourself a moment will help keep your energy up and ensure you don't exhaust yourself.

Engage in Creativity

Lastly, having fun is a great healing tool. Getting creative, for you, might mean making music or simply listening to it. It might mean writing poetry, journaling, or even reading a novel. Engaging your brain in creative and artistic endeavors has been proven to improve physiological and psychological outcomes in people.

You can try art therapy or be completely casual about your creativity and do it alone. What matters is that you engage with anything creative that feels positive for you.

SELF-HYPNOSIS

Have you ever become engrossed in a book? Or were you so engrossed in a movie that time seemed to fly by? If so, you may have been subjected to a common type of hypnosis known as the "everyday trance" by many practitioners.

Hypnosis is a natural state that we enter many times during the day—whenever we become intensely focused on something. The capacity to focus on anything at will is a valuable skill to have, and it provides the foundation for a self-hypnosis practice. This chapter covers how to use self-hypnosis, as well as some of the advantages of doing so.

What Is Self-Hypnosis?
Self-hypnosis involves becoming highly focused and absorbed in the experience while giving yourself positive suggestions about ways to reach your goals. Self-hypnosis is an individual practice, unlike when you are working with a therapist. It can be a most empowering practice as you learn to wield better control over your thoughts and reactions while enjoying the physical and emotional benefits of the relaxation that is typical of self-hypnosis techniques.

What *Can* a Person Accomplish with Self-Hypnosis?

What can humans accomplish if they're in the "right" frame of mind? When people are focused and motivated to accomplish a goal, and most effectively use their abilities, they are at the peak of their personal power. To use that power to learn new skills more easily, perform athletic feats, be more creative, tolerate pain, and face the unknown with greater confidence, are just a few of the infinite examples of the value of self-hypnosis. Self-hypnosis is a means of learning to focus yourself, motivate yourself, be more self-aware, and make the best use of your innate skills. If you think about it, when you see other people do amazing things, they're usually intensely focused on what they're doing and what they're trying to accomplish. Self-hypnosis is all about developing and using your focus in a goal-directed fashion.

Is Self-Hypnosis the *Same as* Meditation?

Self-hypnosis is very similar to meditation in that both involve entering a calm and relaxed state. The main difference is that when people practice self-hypnosis, they tend to have a specific goal in mind—something that will improve them and their quality of life in some way. In a typical meditation practice there is no particular goal, just an easy acceptance of wherever the mind goes without judgment or intention. Both meditation and self-hypnosis have the potential to promote physical and mental health in parallel ways, thus highlighting the merits of learning to develop and use focus meaningfully.

HOW TO HYPNOTIZE YOURSELF

The steps for doing self-hypnosis are listed below. Hypnosis is completely safe, and you will remain in complete control throughout. It is, after all, *your* experience. Simply count to five and instruct yourself to re-alert to terminate the hypnosis session at any point. We'll go through each of these processes in further depth.

- Find a comfortable place to relax and get comfortable
- Relax using hypnotic induction (e.g., progressive muscle relaxation)
- Introduce a suggestion
- Return to your usual level of alertness

1. Find a Comfortable Place

First, make sure you feel physically comfortable as this will help you relax. Sit in a soft chair with your legs and feet uncrossed. You may also lie down although this method may cause you to simply fall sleep. Loosen any tight clothing and avoid eating large meals, so you don't feel bloated and uncomfortable. Ensure that you're not interrupted for the duration of your session.

2. Relax Using Hypnotic Induction

Enter the hypnotic state with a common technique known as progressive muscle relaxation. With this, focus awareness upon any tension stored in parts of the body, and release tension sequentially. Begin with your hands and arms; move down to your back, shoulders, and neck; then, concentrate on your stomach and chest followed by your legs and feet. Visualize the tension dissolving or evaporating, or slowly tense your muscles before relaxing them. The feeling of deep, pleasant, comfortable relaxation is an excellent starting point to begin self-hypnosis.

3. Introduce a Suggestion

In the focused and relaxed state of hypnosis, you can pay deeper and fuller attention to the suggestions you want to give yourself for self-improvement. These can be simple but clear statements you offer yourself about what you might do differently or how you might react differently in some challenging situation or how you might come to think differently about yourself or some circumstance. These "post-hypnotic suggestions" (meaning suggestions that can take effect after your self-hypnosis session is finished) can help you achieve your goals. Some common examples of goals addressed in self-hypnosis include:

- Improving confidence and self-esteem
- Overcoming anxiety
- Quitting smoking
- Overcoming addiction
- Quashing fears and phobias
- Visualizing a goal or action
- Sleeping better

This is a short list, but suggestions can focus on any area of your life in which you hope to initiate a mental shift. Examples of post-hypnotic suggestions in the form of affirmations, a common self-hypnosis approach, include:

- I accept myself for who I am.
- I eat three healthy meals per day.
- I am confident and assertive when speaking to others.

- I feel calm, confident, and relaxed.
- I find it easy to stop smoking..

4. Return to Your Usual Level of Alertness

After providing the suggestions, you can become more alert and aware by counting to five while telling yourself you are becoming aware of your surroundings. At the count of five, you can open your eyes and stretch out your arms and legs and move on with your day.

TIPS FOR HYPNOTIC SUGGESTIONS

When making suggestions during self-hypnosis in step three, follow these tips:

- Speak with Conviction: Imagine the words being spoken gently but with resolution, and ensure the tone is reassuring, confident, and positive.

- Phrase Suggestions in the Present Tense. The suggestion "I am confident" will be more effective than "I will be confident" as the the present tense and is more certain.

- Make Suggestions Positive: For example, "I am at peace" is better than "I am not stressed." Talk to yourself about what you do want, not what you don't want.

- Make Suggestions Realistic: Avoid over-ambitious suggestions such as "I will lose a lot of weight quickly." Instead, focus on smaller and more specific goals such as "I will eat more vegetables and exercise more."

- Repeat the Suggestions: State the suggestions many times during the hypnosis. Repetition of an idea can help drive home the point.

Using Imagery and Action in Self-Hypnosis

Adding imagery to the post-hypnotic suggestions can improve the hypnosis. You may also engage your sense of taste, touch, and smell. For example, to help overcome anxiety you could imagine:

- Sitting in a place that brings you feelings of calm, such as the beach on a warm day.
- Seeing a hot air balloon and placing your worries into the basket, then watching them float away.
- Clearing an overgrown patch of brambles and feeling more robust and more in control as you go.

Adding in action steps—what you'll do differently to improve things—is also helpful to successful self-hypnosis.

Self-Hypnosis or In-Person Hypnotherapy?

There are many advantages to self-hypnosis. It is entirely portable, and with practice, you may be able to quickly bring yourself to a state of focused relaxation very quickly.

It can, however, be challenging to learn, especially the ability to relax and focus the mind while giving oneself instructions. For this reason, many people choose to use in-person hypnotherapy.

Hypnotherapy is simply the act of applying hypnosis as a therapeutic, such as to relieve pain, anxiety, or sleeplessness.

A trained hypnotherapist will take you through a similar process to the above, giving you positive suggestions to help improve your specific concern.

A third option is to use hypnotherapy apps. These apps combine the best of both worlds. They're lower in cost than in-person hypnotherapy and can be done on demand (anywhere, anytime) but are created by real hypnotherapists and based on real clinical studies.

Self-Hypnosis in Medicine

There are remarkable examples that showcase how effective self-hypnosis can be. Take the documented case of Victor Rausch (1980), a dental surgeon who was experienced with hypnotic procedures. When required surgery to remove his gallbladder, Rausch used self-hypnosis as his only anesthesia.

More recently, science has shown training in self-hypnosis may help patients overcome a range of clinical conditions. These include:

- Anxiety: Patients who have undergone heart surgery show lower levels of depress and fatigue after learning self-hypnosis techniques. A study in children with cancer showed less and surgery-related anxiety and behavioral distress after learning self-hypnosis.

- Pain: Patients with multiple sclerosis (MS) reported lower levels of chronic pain after learning self-hypnosis techniques than those who did not. Further, a study in children showed functional abdominal pain resolved in three weeks following a single session of self-hypnosis.

- Tension Headaches: In children and adolescents, self-hypnosis training reduced the frequency of tension headaches. Another study in adults showed long-term headache pain reduction from self-hypnosis.

- Chronic Dyspnea: In adults with breathing difficulty at rest, a single training in self-hypnosis resolved symptoms in thirteen of sixteen patients within one month.

- Irritable Bowel Syndrome: Patients with IBS have been shown to be able to improve IBS symptoms as much as the gold standard Low FODMAP elimination diet.

Tips for Improving Self-Hypnosis

- Have a Goal in Mind: Before starting self-hypnosis, make sure you have a clear goal in mind (e.g., lowering stress). This will ensure each session is focused and productive.

- Schedule Time for Self-Hypnosis: The hardest part of self-hypnosis can be getting started. It may work best to set aside a time each day for self-hypnosis and write it in your schedule. Self-hypnosis can be performed during the day, or at night before, you sleep.

- Continue the Practice: Like riding a bike, it takes time to learn self-hypnosis. With practice and instruction, you will learn to more quickly enter a state of trance. You will also learn a broader range of hypnotic suggestions to improve the outcome.

PREPARING FOR HYPNOSIS

Get into Comfortable Clothing

It's pretty hard entering any kind of deep, relaxed state when all you can think about is the waistband of your jeans cutting off your circulation. So, take this as an excuse to throw on some sweats. You want absolutely nothing distracting you. Make sure the temperature is suitable, too. Have a blanket or a sweater ready if you run on the chilly side. Sometimes, feeling warm can be very comforting, too.

Go to a Quiet Room and Get Comfy.

Although some people prefer to lie down, you are more susceptible to sleep when supine. Whether you sit or lie, ensure that you don't cross your legs or any part of your body. You may be in this position for a while and this could end up being uncomfortable.

Make Sure You're Not Going to Be Disturbed

No self-hypnosis is effective if it gets interrupted by a phone call, a pet, or a kid. Turn off your phone (and the alerts), lock the door, and sequester yourself. This is you time.

The amount of time you want to dedicate to this is up to you. Most prefer to remain in the hypnotic state for fifteen or twenty minutes, but you should also allow for time to get into and out of the desired state, too.

Figure Out Your Hypnosis Goals

Are you doing it just to relax? For self-improvement? To train your brain? If you're doing it to achieve a greater end (weight loss, quitting smoking, etc.), prepare a list of affirmations. Self-hypnosis can be used for relaxation, sure, but it can enhance your life in far more profound ways. Many use it to achieve their goals, alter their mindset, or as a means of general positive reinforcement or motivation. Here are some examples of affirmations you could try:

- Suppose you want to quit a bad habit, something to the point is the most effective. Think along the lines of, "I choose no longer to smoke. Cigarettes have no appeal to me."

- If you want to think more positively, aim for something like, "I am capable of whatever I set my mind to. I am in control, and I am valuable."

- If you want to reach a specific goal, like weight loss, say it in the present tense: "I am eating healthy. I am losing my excess weight. My clothes feel better, and I feel better."

- These are statements you will be reciting to yourself when you're under hypnosis. Again, it's up to you, but many find them life-affirming and highly effective.

ENTERING HYPNOSIS

Close your eyes and focus on removing any fear, tension, or anxiety from your thoughts. You might find it challenging not to think when you first start. Your opinions may keep interrupting you. Don't attempt to push the ideas out when this happens. Observe them objectively before letting them go.

Alternatively, some people like to focus on a specific point on the wall. It may be a smudge, a corner, or just about anywhere you want it to be. Concentrate on your eyelids while focusing on the subject. Remind yourself that they're growing heavier and heavier, and when you can't keep them open any longer, close them.

Recognize the tension in your body.

Beginning with your toes, and imagine the tension slowly falling away from your body and vanishing. Imagine it freeing each body part one at a time, starting with your toes and working its way up your body. Visualize each part of your body becoming lighter and lighter as the tension is removed.

Relax your toes, then your feet. Continue with your calves, thighs, hips, stomach, and so on, until you've relaxed each portion, including your face and head. Using imagery techniques of something you find comforting or soothing, such as water (feel the water rushing over your feet and ankles, cleansing them of tension) can be effective as well.

Take slow, deep breaths.

When you exhale, see the tension and negativity leaving in a dark cloud. As you inhale, see the air returning as a bright force filled with life and energy.

At this point, you can use visualization as you so choose. Think of a lemon and cut it in half in your mind. Imagine the juices oozing out over your fingers. Place it in your mouth.

What's your reaction? How does it feel, taste, and smell? Then, move onto more meaningful visions. Imagine your bills blowing away in the breeze. Imagine running off those pounds. Get as detailed as possible. Always think of your five senses.

Appreciate the fact that you are now extremely relaxed.

Imagine you're at the top of a flight of ten stairs that are at the fifth step, and start to submerge yourself in water. Picture every detail of this scene from the top to the bottom. Tell yourself that you are going to descend the stairs, counting each step down, starting at ten. Picture each number in your mind. Imagine that each number you count is further down and one step closer to the bottom. After each number, you will feel yourself drifting further and further into deep relaxation.

As you take each step, imagine the feel of the step under your feet. Once you're at the fifth step, imagine and truly feel the refreshing coolness of the water and tell yourself that you are stepping into an oasis of purity and cleanliness. As you begin to descend the last five steps, start to feel the water getting higher and higher up your body. You should now start to feel somewhat numb, and your heart will start to race a bit but notice it and let any qualms about the situation drift away into the water.

Next, you'll feel a floating sensation.

At this point, at the bottom of the water, you shoulddododododon't feel anything—just the sensation of floating freely—You may even feel like you're spinning. If you don't feel as stated above, try again, slower and with a will to grasp what's happening. Once you've achieved this state, you should proceed to address your problems and decide upon what it is you want from where you are.

Now start to narrate what you're doing. Speak in the present and future tense quietly to yourself—as if you're reading it from a page.

Start to picture three boxes under the water that you have to swim to get to. Once you've found the boxes, open them slowly, one at a time, and narrate to yourself what's happening when you open the box (e.g., "As I open the box I feel a radiant light engulf me; I feel it becoming a part of me. This light is the newfound confidence that I can never lose, as it is now a part of me"). Then, proceed to the next box.

Again, you should avoid using statements with a negative connotation, such as "I don't want to be tired and irritable." Instead, say, "I'm becoming calm and relaxed." Examples of positive statements include: "I'm strong and slender," "I'm successful and positive," and, if you have pain, "My back is beginning to feel wonderful." (See warning on pain.

Repeat your statement(s) to yourself as many times as you wish.

Feel free to wander about the water, visualizing yourself emptying boxes, finding treasure (in the form of self-confidence, money, etc.), or simply letting all your tensions disappear. Find areas where the water is cold, hot, or full of wildlife. Let your imagination go.

Get ready to exit your hypnotic state.

With each step you take, feel the water becoming lower and lower until you have once again reached that fifth step. Once you're out of the water and find yourself on the sixth step, you may start to feel heavy—as if there's a weight on your chest. Merely wait on the step until this feeling passes, constantly repeating your statements above.

Once it passes, continues up the stairs, visualizing each step by its number, feeling the steps underneath you. Will yourself to carry on up the stairs.

For the record, this water visualization isn't your only option if you come up with another scenario that you prefer, use it! It's just as good, if not better, since it works for you.

Once you've ascended, give yourself a few moments before opening your eyes.

You may want to visualize yourself opening a door to the outside world. Do this slowly and imagine the light that pours in through the doorway; this should make your eyes open naturally. If you need to, count down from ten, telling yourself that once you finish, your eyes will open.

Take your time getting up. Then, tell yourself, "Wide awake, wide awake," or something you're used to, in order to wake up. This will put your mind back in the conscious state, bringing you back to reality.

ENHANCING YOUR EXPERIENCE

Mean It

No self-hypnosis or mantra will manifest itself in real life if you don't actually mean it. For this to be effective, you have to believe in yourself and your actions. And why not? If you do mean it, it could work.

If the first time doesn't seem effective, don't write it off automatically. Some things take time to get used to and to get good at. Come back to it in a few days and revisit the experiences. You may be surprised.

Open your mind. You have to believe there is a possibility of this working in order for it to work. Any skepticism on your part will impede your progress.

Test Yourself Physically

If you need proof you're in a trance, there are exercises you can do! Anything that can be seen or felt in your body can work. Try these ideas on for size:

- Entwine your fingers. Keep them together throughout your trance, telling yourself that they're stuck together—almost as if they're covered in glue. Then, try to take them apart. If you find you can't . . . proof!

- Think of one arm getting heavier and heavier. You don't need to consciously pick one; your brain will do this for you. Imagine a book on top of it, holding it down. Then, try to lift it up. Can you?

Visualize Situations

Whatever it is you're working toward—be it confidence, weight loss, or positive thinking—visualize yourself in the situation acting as you'd like to react or being as you'd like to be if you want to be thinner, imagine yourself sliding into your skinny jeans with ease, modeling in the mirror, and smiling at your beautiful body. The endorphin rush alone will be worth it!

Many use hypnosis to get over certain issues like shyness. You don't have to attack the shyness head on; something related will do. Simply imagining yourself going about the world with your head high, smiling, and making eye contact can be the first step toward a more extroverted you.

Use outside stimuli to assist you. Some people like music to help them enter hypnosis. There are a bunch of hypnosis tracks available online that are just for this purpose. If a certain scene—water, the rainforest, etc.—would help, you have it at your fingertips!

Timers can be helpful, too. Some find that getting out of the trance is difficult, and they lose track of time. If you don't want to accidentally spend hours hypnotized, you can use a timer. Just make sure it has a soothing tone.

Use It to Better Yourself.

Find a goal that you'd like to achieve and concentrate on it during your relaxed state. Think of the person you'd like to be and be that person. Hypnosis is great for a deep, deep meditation, but its better in that it can be used for a bigger, better purpose. Many people find that they emerge more positive and with a sense of purpose afterward. Take advantage of that possibility!

There is no wrong way to go about this. Whether it's kicking a bad habit, having focus in your work life, or just changing your thinking, hypnosis can help. Getting rid of the stressors in your life is an integral part of being the person you want to become and this will help. And the more you do it, the better and more natural it'll feel.

TIPS

1. Some find that imagining yourself in a peaceful natural setting will relax your mind sufficiently before counting down. For instance, you may imagine yourself wandering through a forest, smelling the trees and hearing the wind. Alternatively, you could imagine yourself walking along the ocean shore and feeling the grit of the sand beneath your feet, the excellent water washing against your ankle,s and sounds of the surf.

2. Know that you never lose control during hypnosis. You are always in control.

3. Have an idea of how you will present your suggestions to yourself before you lie down and are relaxed; otherwise, it may interrupt your hypnotic state.

4. Another way to relax your muscles is to physically tense and hold for ten seconds before releasing; you should feel as well as imagine the tension leaving.

5. You were writing out your suggestions before induction can be very effective, as a visual list of what you choose to work on can sometimes be more easily remembered than even carefully assembled thoughts.

6. Don't force yourself or think about it, and it will be much easier. Also, this is a good way to get to sleep

7. Remember that hypnosis is natural, so it should not interfere with any religious or spiritual beliefs.

8. No one can hypnotize you against your will. You can't even hypnotize yourself unless you're fully committed to it.

9. If you can't sleep after you count down from ten, allow your mind to remain in this pleasantly relaxed state and keep your eyes closed. At the same time, you are lying down, and you'll sleep much easier.

10. For those of you who like to meditate but can't sit still long enough, just use this as a form of meditation but insert a period of time in between counting down from ten and counting back up to ten.

11. Don't try to put yourself into a hypnotic state while you are driving or operating heavy machinery.

12. Don't worry. You can't get stuck in hypnotic trance. Hypnosis is natural and you "slip" in and out of it daily.

13. If you are struggling, try visiting a hypnotherapist or buying a recording in order to experience hypnosis. When

you have experienced it once or twice, you'll better know the state of mind you're aiming to achieve.

Self-hypnosis is a powerful tool to improve your mind. It's a highly safe technique that can increase self-esteem and confidence, assertiveness, and relaxation. Self-hypnosis can also be used during difficult times to help improve symptoms of medical conditions such as irritable bowel syndrome, anxiety, pain, and headaches.

Materialism

REAL-LIFE STORY
by Annette add

I remember the first time that I overate. I was only eight years old and stuffed myself to oblivion at a buffet. After eating, I immediately got a sense of calmness and comfort from being that complete. My life was hectic. My dad had just diagnosed with cancer, my mom had to start working, and my whole world was upside down.

I began to escape more and more with food. My overeating eventually transitioned into full-blown binge eating. Around twelve years old, I started to gain weight rapidly. By twenty, I weighed my heaviest at 261 pounds.

I was miserable, a tight size twenty-two quickly approaching a size twenty-four. As my pants size continued to accelerate past my age, I knew I had to do something to get my eating under control. I consider this my first rock-bottom. I started a popular low-carb plan and dropped my weight exceptionally fast.

Unfortunately, I wasted almost a decade of my life up and down the scale. No matter how hard I tried, I never get in control of my eating.

I yo-yo dieted so drastically that I had four different sizes of clothes in my closet at any given time. It's a rollercoaster ride that I wouldn't wish on my worst enemy. My pursuit to be thin eventually led me down a dark path to try anything to stop the weight gain. By my mid-twenties, I was engulfed in a severe eating disorder. I was either binging, restricting, or doing something unhealthy to erase a binge. It was a nightmarish existence.

Fast-forward a few years, shortly after I moved to Los Angeles, and I was on yet another starvation diet. I lost twelve pounds in a month, and after getting a couple of days off work, I decided to celebrate my success with a "cheat meal." You can probably guess what happened; it permitted me to binge for two days. I got on the scale and gained ten pounds in two days.

Back then, I was oblivious to water weight. Still, either way, it was incredibly heartbreaking to see that massive fluctuation in weight after trying so hard to get my weight down. This was my second rock-bottom. The struggle was is emotionally exhausting. I couldon't do this anymore. I was done dieting, but I didn't know where to turn.

In the past, I had tried traditional therapy, support groups, every diet imaginable—even overeaters anonymous—and nothing seemed to help.

There had to be an answer out there. I briefly entertained the thought of embracing my body, but I knew deep down inside I would not be happy fat. I went on a research frenzy to try to find the answer. Then, I came across my first hypnotherapist's website. I'll admit, I was a little skeptical at first. However, I was willing to try anything to overcome this crippling part of my life, so I scheduled a hypnosis appointment. At the time, I had no idea how much this decision would impact the course of my life.

After about three weeks of working on my therapist's hypnosis plan and listening to her recordings, I noticed a significant difference in my cravings and my compulsions around food.

My bulimic behavior disappeared the quickest. I've never had another episode since: the portion control and relationship with food took a little longer. Around month six, I felt like a normal person around food for the first time in my adult life. After experiencing this freedom, I felt so much better, and I wanted to pay it forward.

I wanted everyone to experience this freedom from any cycle they're trapped in that's destroying their life. I changed my career focus entirely and began to study hypnotherapy. A year later, I was a certified hypnotherapist working in the field. Every day, I feel like I'm fulfilling my true purpose. The mind is tricky. We gets into subconscious loops, and our behavior ends up on autopilot. Maybe you can identify in your own life where you have some destructive behaviors or habits that you would like to get rid of (Annette).

Have you tried and failed? The reason you can't overcome these behaviors is that 88 percent of your mind is subconscious.

It's easy to see why 12 percent of your conscious effort gets beat out by the more dominant subconscious mind.

Most of the time, these behaviors and auto-pilot loops begin in childhood or adolescence. These patterns become known in your mind as safe. Like in the example of my own life, my mind started to associate eating large quantities of food with safety and comfort. This set the groundwork for a lifelong struggle with my weight. Another common example is smoking. I want everyone to experience the change they desire.

Life is too precious to spend it struggling. I wasted too much time stuck in a cycle that took away my joy and my focus in life. I want you to know that you have the power inside you to change anything you want.

With a few mental shifts using hypnosis, you can create new habits and behaviors that'll create your best life.

Materialisim

CONCLUSION

While not everyone reacts to hypnosis in the same way, it has been shown to help some people build the willpower and capacity to break away from specific behavior patterns, even when they return to waking consciousness.

Essentially, materialism causes you to be less happy, less grateful, less friendly, less likable, less empathic, and less purposeful. However, it makes you more antisocial, egoistic, incompetent, and unfriendly—and it makes people think you're an asshole on top of that.

Patients are more likely to stay in a treatment program, attend meetings, and work with sponsors to understand their addictions better. In a nutshell, it can make patients more eager and open to many aspects of the addiction treatment procedure.

Hopefully, you've realized that getting rid of materialistic tendencies is an intelligent move. The good news is that anyone can overcome materialism with a bit of patience and the appropriate tactics.

Additionally, the pain-relieving properties of hypnosis can be utilized to reduce physical barriers to recovery, including withdrawal, anxiety, muscle tension, spasms, and pain.

Our health and well-being are threatened by materialism. It has been demonstrated to drain our happiness but our relationships in jeopardy and make us less sociable, likable, and empathic while also making us nervous, sad, and selfish.

In ads, TV shows, and other media, we're inundated with materialism-inducing messages and unending celebrations glorifying the rich, handsome, and famous.

We must counterbalance society's conditioning and discover methods to overcome materialism if we're to be happy and fulfilled.

One final point to consider? Hypnosis, despite its potential, is not a cure. There is no such thing as an instant fix in a single session. It isn't practical for everyone, either. It can, however, be a beneficial aid in the process of tackling the complexities and challenges of addiction for certain people.

Materialisim
My-mindguide.com

DON'T FORGET

If you enjoyed this title and would like to read about other topics that have changed my life, please check out my new books on Amazon or my website: www.my-mindguide.com.

Also, let's stay connected on social media. Please drop a line on Facebook or Instagram, and stay tuned for updates! You're welcome to share your thoughts with me directly as well: gassner@my-mindguide.com. In return, I'll send you a gorgeous infographic that you can cut out and frame.

Also, please leave a review on Amazon, as this will help me reach an even broader audience. Thank you so much for your time, insight, and an undying hunger for knowledge!

I want to say thank you to all of my colleagues, clients, friends, and family members, who have all contributed to what I am now.

I also want to thank Gabriel Palacios, a Swiss bestseller author, the king of hypnotherapy. He taught this old fox new tricks, letting me deep-dive into the mystery of hypnotherapy. I learned so much along the journey that I'm now a certified master-hypnosis coach and conversation coach myself!

Furthermore, I want to thank you to the fantastic teachers of SAMYANA/Bali who trained me to become a certified yoga and meditation teacher.

Last but not least, I give a special thanks to my master-teacher Eckhard Wunderle, who's close to a saint to me. He introduced me to the world of meditation and let me discover all the wonders it has to offer. I couldn't be more proud of receiving my meditation teacher certification directly from him at the Institut für Spirituelle Psychologie.

Peace, love, and happiness to all of you—till next time!

Authors portrait

Kurt Friedrich Gassner has worn many hats throughout his lifetime, including but not limited to serial entrepreneur, Creative Director, Meditation Teacher, Licensed Hypnotherapist, and more recently, self-improvement author. Leveraging his treasure trove of experiences and in-depth knowledge of psychology, he provides his readers with the tools they need to unlock their infinite potential.

As a prolific self-help writer, Kurt has authored the following books: *The Art of Forgiveness, Lie or Die, Soul-Match, Can You Inherit a Poisoned Mind?* and *The Power of Poverty*. He also authored a best-selling children's book in German-speaking countries and has over 20 books underway.

When it comes to enduring success, Kurt understands that financial prosperity isn't the only aspect one should strive for. He may be a self-made millionaire, but what really transformed his life is mastering his unconscious mind. Perseverance, personal power, self-awareness, and learning from past mistakes have all been key ingredients to bringing his dreams to fruition—and he strives to impart that wisdom onto others through his writing.

During his spare time, Kurt Friedrich Gassner is either traveling across the globe, golfing, biking in the Alps, hiking, or spending quality time with his loved ones. For the last 37 years, he has been happily married and he is the father of two successful children. Presently, he resides in both Munich, Germany, and Kirchberg, Austria.

My-mindguide.com
An inspirational book to overcoming past trauma
POWER OF FORGIVENESS
PRACTICING SELF-FORGIVENESS
KURT GASSNER

My-mindguide.com
A practical guide for self healing and overcome past traumas
The Art Of FORGIVNESS
KURT GASSNER

My-mindguide.com
Match Me If You Can
How We Can Swipe Without Getting Hurt
KURT GASSNER

My-mindguide.com
SOUL MATCH
PREPARE YOUR BRAIN WITH HYPNOSIS TO FIND SOMEONE
WHO'S REALLY RIGHT FOR YOU
KURT GASSNER

OTHER BOOKS BY THE AUTHOR

OTHER BOOKS BY THE AUTHOR

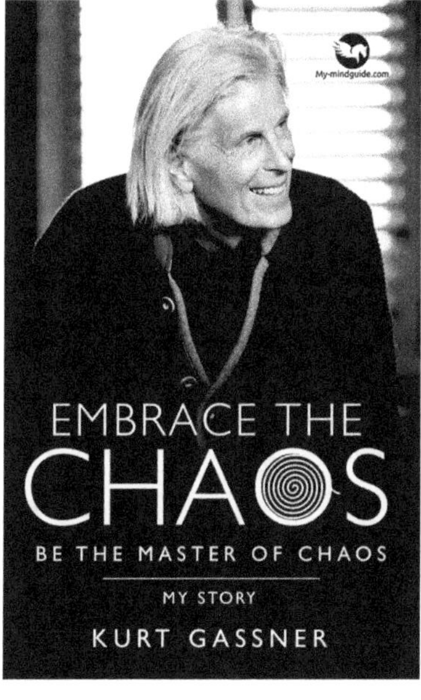

OTHER BOOKS BY THE AUTHOR

OTHER BOOKS BY THE AUTHOR

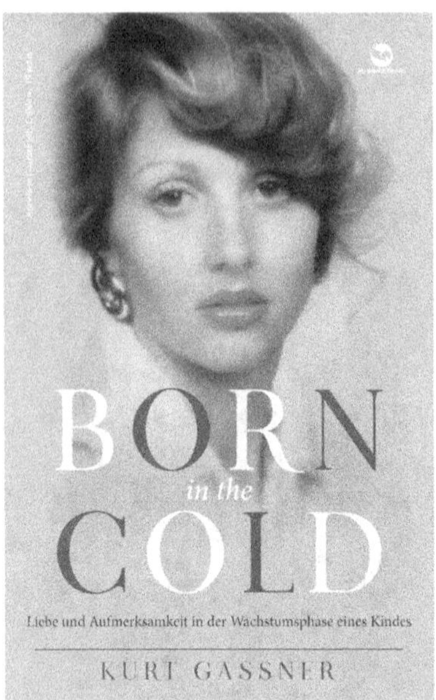

BORN
in the
COLD
Liebe und Aufmerksamkeit in der Wachstumsphase eines Kindes
KURT GASSNER

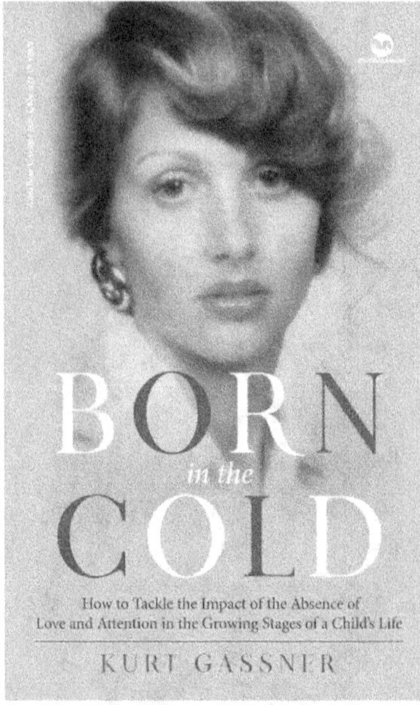

BORN
in the
COLD
How to Tackle the Impact of the Absence of
Love and Attention in the Growing Stages of a Child's Life
KURT GASSNER

SOPHIAS WUNDERWELT
10 ERZÄHLUNGEN
KURT GASSNER

SOPHIA'S WONDERWORLD
10 TALES
KURT GASSNER

BESTSELLING AUTHOR OF
The Art Of
FORGIVNESS
AMAZON #1 BESTSELLER
My-mindguide.com
A practical guide for self healing and overcome past traumas
The Art Of
FORGIVNESS
KURT GASSNER
The Art Of
FORGIVNESS
KURT GASSNER

9 783987 939990